# INTER

**International Terrorism in** **1989**

## JCSS Publications

JCSS publications present the findings and assessments of the Center's research staff. Each paper represents the work of a single investigator or a team. Such teams may also include research fellows who are not members of the Center's staff. Views expressed in the Center's publications are those of the authors and do not necessarily reflect the views of the Center, its trustees, officers, or other staff members or organizations and individuals that support its research. Thus the publication of a work by JCSS signifies that it is deemed worthy of public consideration but does not imply endorsement of conclusions or recommendations.

Editor
Aharon Yariv

Executive Editor
Joseph Alpher

# JCSS project on low intensity warfare

# INTER

International Terrorism in **1989**

*anat kurz*

*maskit burgin* • *michal cadouri*

*sofia kotzer* • *yoel kozak*

*orit shahmon* • *david tal* • *yael treiber*

Routledge
Taylor & Francis Group

LONDON AND NEW YORK

First published 1990 by Westview Press

Published 2018 by Routledge
2 Park Square, Milton Park, Abingdon, Oxon OX14 4RN
52 Vanderbilt Avenue, New York, NY 10017

*Routledge is an imprint of the Taylor & Francis Group, an informa business*

Library of Congress ISSN: 86-645044

ISBN 13: 978-0-367-01239-7 (hbk)
ISBN 13: 978-0-367-16226-9 (pbk)

# Table of Contents

                                                             Page

1.   Introduction                                              3

2.   International Terrorism in 1989: Main
     Features                                                  6
     by Anat Kurz

3.   Statistical Tables and Figures                           17
     by Sofia Kotzer

4.   Shi'ite International Terrorism                           36
     by Maskit Burgin

5.   The International Dimension of PFLP-GC
     Activity                                                 61
     by David Tal

6.   Palestinian International Terrorism in 1989              78
     by Anat Kurz

7.   Chronology of Main International Terrorist
     Incidents in 1989                                        87
     by Orit Shahmon


Appendix: Organizations Responsible for
     International Terrorist Incidents                        106

# Acknowledgments

InTer is the annual survey of the Jaffee Center's Project on Low Intensity Warfare. Compiling it is a demanding task that calls for intensive efforts by each and every member of the Project's staff. They deserve credit not only for their achievements as analysts of raw data, but also for their valuable teamwork.

Many additional people assisted in producing this report. The JCSS Information Center, directed by Moshe Grundman, supplied the media clippings and other sources of information that formed the basis for data collection and analysis. Special thanks are due to Joseph Alpher, Deputy Head and Executive Editor of JCSS, whose professional contribution was critical in publishing the survey.

A.K.
Spring 1990

# 1. INTRODUCTION

This report surveys international terrorism in 1989. It is the sixth annual survey of its kind published by the Jaffee Center for Strategic Studies' Project on Low Intensity Warfare. As in previous years' reports, the current survey contains statistical data that delineate various aspects of international terrorism, as well as brief articles that analyze major current issues in international terrorism. This year the articles include a discussion of the international dimension of the activity of the Popular Front for the Liberation of Palestine-General Command (PFLP-GC), a review of Shi'ite international terrorism, and a survey of Palestinian international terrorism in 1989. A chronology of significant international terrorist events in 1989 is included, as well as extensive tables and figures, and a glossary of terrorist organizations active in the international arena during the period under review.

The report is based on data collected, collated and computerized at the JCSS Project on Low Intensity Warfare. That project was established in 1979. Its aims are to maintain a data base on terrorism around the world, to issue periodic situation reports, and to conduct studies analyzing the processes, trends and phenomenon of terrorism.

The Project's data base on terrorism contains three files:

*Terrorist Events*--a systematic cataloguing of international as well as domestic terrorist incidents that take place in most parts of the world;

*Terrorist Groups*--a continually updated collection of information on terrorist groups around the world, according to a predetermined list of detailed categories; and

*Countries' Attitudes to Terrorism*--monitored and documented information on the various forms of state

3

support for terrorist groups, as well as on the methods states use to combat terrorism.

For purposes of data collection, a **terrorist group** is defined as an organization other than a state (although it may enjoy state support and/or act in the service of a state) that resorts to the systematic use of violence in order to achieve political ends. A **terrorist incident** is any violent activity conducted by a non-state organization in order to attain political objectives. An **international terrorist incident** (in contrast to a domestic incident) is defined as a terrorist incident that in some way involves more than one state. In addition to these categories, the JCSS data base monitors international terrorist activity conducted by direct emissaries of states on foreign territory.

The data base relies mainly on information from the mass communications media (primarily dailies, weeklies and periodicals), professional publications, and government releases. Media information concerning terrorism is problematic for two reasons: first, coverage of events, especially those taking place in remote parts of the world, is sometimes deficient--although international terrorist incidents are generally covered better than domestic ones, and terrorist activity involving western interests receives particularly good coverage. The second point is related to the clandestine nature of terrorist activity. Information about the actual perpetrators and their intentions is sometimes incomplete, contradictory or simply absent. However, there is usually no doubt regarding the very occurrence and the physical results of an incident.

As mentioned above, international terrorist incidents are defined as those events in which more than one country is involved. Nevertheless, in the present report, as in previous ones, we excluded incidents that formed part of a struggle conducted by rebels against a foreign army in their own or their host country--such as attacks perpetrated by Shi'ites and Palestinians against the IDF in Lebanon. Inclusion of violent events

4

associated with struggles of this sort would considerably distort the picture of international terrorism.

The statistics also refer to incidents carried out by states' agents when the attacks targeted either the public-at-large, or individuals not associated with a dissident organization involved in terrorism. Attacks against members of terrorist groups are considered part of a counterterrorism effort conducted by the state, and are excluded from this report.

# 2. INTERNATIONAL TERRORISM IN 1989: MAIN FEATURES

International terrorism refers to incidents involving more than one state. A salient characteristic of terrorist assaults that involve nationals or interests of several countries, has been that the major part of the assaults targeted foreign objectives within the borders of the perpetrators' own country. In 1989, attacks of this kind comprised 78.4 percent of international terrorism. Infiltration by terrorists for the purpose of carrying out cross-border attacks constituted nine percent of the total incidents, while attacks carried out beyond national borders against either objectives of the terrorists' own nationality or foreign targets, comprised about 12.6 percent of total incidents. This feature of international terrorism, which has been constant throughout the years, apparently reflects logistical feasibilities and practical considerations.

Various factors appear to precipitate changes in activity of diverse terrorist organizations, in the selection of objectives for operations, and in the scope and volume of activity in the different spheres. Some of these reflect the impact of political changes, or countermeasures practiced by the affected states, while others are primarily linked with intra-group processes. Taken together, these factors form global patterns.

The statistics surveyed in this report present common denominators and main features of international terrorism worldwide. Hence the criteria used to illustrate global trends ignore, to a great extent, the specific causes that bring about shifts in the activity of individuals and organizations.

The volume of international terrorism in 1989 remained about the same as in the previous year. A total of 406 attacks was carried out internationally, comprising a decrease of about 6 percent compared with 1988. A single salient feature of international terrorism in

1989 was a decrease in the number of victims. Otherwise, there was no significant change with regard to the major features of international activity: preferred tactics, objectives for assault, and operational venues. Rather, as in previous years, the phenomenon gained attention as a result of a few dramatic incidents and their consequences.

Particularly notable in 1989 were several phenomena that were associated in some way with Shi'ite terrorism. In February a death sentence was issued in Tehran against the British author Salman Rushdie, author of *The Satanic Verses*, a book that enraged the Muslim world. This was accompanied by threats to carry out the sentence, and concrete warnings against publishing houses involved with the book. Actual attacks perpetrated around the globe against this backdrop, however, were mostly minor. The affair demonstrated the potential of terrorism--even in the form of a threat--to generate public concern and affect international developments.

Another issue that again captured public attention in 1989 concerned the ongoing affair of western hostages held by Hizballah in Lebanon. Here developments were not initiated by the terrorists, but rather by Israel's capture of one of the leaders of the organization. This step, taken to obtain leverage in negotiating the release of Israeli soldiers held captive by Hizballah, restored the hostage issue to the headlines at a time when world public interest had declined significantly, and the primary western government seeking the hostages' release, the US, preferred a low-key approach.

The explosion in September of a UTA airliner over Niger, thought to have been directed by Iran and perpetrated in cooperation with Palestinian extremists, did not generate the kind of intense interest in uncovering its perpetrators that one might have anticipated. Time and again it emerges that the nature of incidents, their frequency and even lethality, are not always dominant in generating international diplomatic tension and broad public reaction. Indeed, the UTA incident offered a further demonstration of the public's widely recognized inclination to be influenced by governmental response in its reaction to international terrorism.

## Tactical Preferences

Together, the three most popular tactics throughout the years--bombing, armed assault and kidnapping--accounted for 90.2 percent of international terrorism carried out in 1989 worldwide.

Bombing attacks have been the most common terrorist tactic. In 1989, incidents of this type accounted for 49 percent of the total number of international terrorist incidents. This tactic has obviously remained the simplest in operational terms, and the least risky for conveying a message and attracting public awareness. Yet when used in a sophisticated manner, bombing can be a highly demonstrative and destructive practice.

Thus, midair explosions of airliners have proved one of the most spectacular terrorist tactics, and account for a considerable share of the victims of all attacks. The most lethal terrorist incident carried out in the period under review was the September 19 explosion in midair over the Sahara Desert in Niger of a UTA airliner, which resulted in the deaths of 171 passengers and crew. In November, an Avianca Airlines plane exploded over Colombia, claiming the lives of 107 passengers and crew. Also in November, an air disaster was prevented when a bomb was safely defused aboard a Saudi airliner flying from Pakistan to Riyadh.

Armed attacks accounted for 35.3 percent of the total of international terrorist incidents in 1989. This indicates an increase compared to the previous year's rates, when attacks of this kind comprised 28.2 percent of the world total. In 1989 specific threats ("if you don't...then...") comprised 6.7 percent of terrorist incidents, while kidnappings comprised 5.9 percent of the total--a decrease compared to the 14.3 percent figure for 1987 and 7.8 percent in 1988.

Sabotage incidents comprised less than one percent of the total. Additional tactics--barricade-hostage assaults, letter bombs, hijackings and poisoning--each accounted for less then one percent of all international terrorism in 1989. Whereas the infrequent use of sabotage apparently attests to the minimal impact anticipated from an incident of this type, reliance on sophisticated and dramatic tactics tends on the whole to be influenced by diverse combinations of practical and political factors. Rates of hijackings, barricade-hostage incidents and abductions have always been low, despite the relatively sensational impact they may have, due to constraints such as an organization's ability to carry out complicated and hazardous operations, its strategic mindset, and the political and physical countermeasures already implemented or expected to be taken by the targeted state or institution.

For details see Figure 1 and Table 3 in Chapter 3.


## Geographical Distribution

In recent years Latin America has been the preferred arena for international terrorist activity. Incidents perpetrated there accounted for 39 percent of the world total for 1989, marking a dramatic increase compared with 1988 (26.5 percent) and 1987 (28.5 percent).

In 1989 Western Europe accounted for 19.7 percent of the total worldwide. This rate marked a decrease compared with 24.2 percent of total international terrorist activity recorded there in 1988, and 23.6 percent in 1987--the years when Western Europe lost its 'traditional' position as the preferred arena for international terrorism. Several factors have accounted for this steady decline. One is a relative decrease in the activity of Middle Eastern terrorist groups for whom Western Europe had formed the principal arena for years: a decline in the activity of Palestinian as well as Shi'ite radicals there, already evident during 1987 and 1988, continued throughout 1989. A second factor has been growing cooperation among European states, accompanied by intensive anti-terrorism measures implemented by states independently. These two factors have been considered vital in reducing the volume of international terrorism on Western European soil. Additional logistical difficulties for European and Middle-Eastern terrorists alike are likely to emerge as a result of the political changes taking place in Eastern Europe, whereby many regimes appear to have changed their policies regarding the sheltering and abetting of terrorists.

In 1989, ten countries were venues for about 55 percent of all international attacks around the globe. These were: Colombia (12.6 percent of the total), Chile, Peru, Pakistan, and Lebanon (between 5 and 6.5 percent of the total each), Spain, Philippines, South Korea, the Federal Republic of Germany, and Turkey (between 3 and 5 percent of the world total each). The role of some of these countries as the scene of international terrorist activity was acquired as a result of concerted waves of assaults perpetrated on their soil against specific targets. In most cases these involved spates of rather minor attacks that went virtually unnoticed by the world public-at-large, although some resulted in loss of life.

Colombia was the most active operational site for terrorists involved in incidents that targeted foreign interests, and the volume of activity there also significantly contributed to Latin America's leading role as a venue for international terrorism. A considerable portion of activity recorded on Colombian soil was carried out by terrorist elements operating against a political backdrop, yet involved in the drug trade. An effort was made to exclude from the statistics incidents carried out on criminal grounds that, while possibly having political ramifications, were not considered politically motivated.

For details see Tables 1, 2 and 3 in Chapter 3.

### Aims of Terrorist Attacks and Specific Targets

Of the 406 international terrorist incidents recorded in 1989, 35.9 percent were directed solely at causing property damage. About 22 percent were aimed at random killing together with property damage, 13.8 percent were aimed at random killing alone, and 7.1 were aimed at assassination. Thus about 43.5 percent of the total incidents (about the same proportion as recorded in 1988), whether successful or thwarted, were intended in some way to cause deaths: 36.4 percent of these intended random killing rather than specific assassination. Overall, the trend of incidents intended to kill over the past four years marks a decline in terrorist lethality compared with 1985, when 52.8 percent of total international incidents were aimed at loss of life.

Returning to 1989, some 58 percent of incidents were related in some way to actual or attempted property damage. Of the total number of international incidents recorded in 1989, 4.4 percent were aimed at political and/or financial extortion, including intended or actual property loss.

In 1989, attacks against political figures constituted about 42.1 percent of all international attacks worldwide. Economic targets--business facilities and personnel--were the second common objective for international terrorism, and accounted for 32 percent of the world total, marking a slight increase compared with the previous year. These were followed by random public and diplomatic targets as the preferred objective for terrorist assaults.

The public-at-large formed the target in 22.6 percent of total actual or intended attacks worldwide. This figure accords with the previous two years' trends (24.7 percent in 1988, 26 percent in 1987), though in 1986 the public-at-large was targeted in only 15.6 percent of the incidents. The targeting of political figures and diplomatic objectives also reflected an extension of the previous year's trend, when an increase in these attacks was evident. In 1989 political and diplomatic targets also exceeded economic objectives, which had been the preferred target for international terrorism for years.

In 1989 only six incidents--1.4 percent of the total--in some way involved the targeting of civil aviation

11

(including one specific threat and another attack that was thwarted). This figure marks a significant decrease compared to the previous year, when aviation comprised the objective of 4.6 percent of all attacks (20 incidents in all). Yet two of the incidents recorded in 1989 resulted in a considerable share of the year's total victims.

For details see Tables 4, 9, and 12 in Chapter 3.


## The Victims

A total of 131 incidents recorded in 1989 involved human victims: killed, wounded or kidnapped. This overall figure accounted for 32 percent of the total number of incidents and corresponded with the previous year's statistics. All told, 553 people were killed in international terrorist incidents in 1989, 278 of them in the UTA and Avianca midair explosions, while 499 people were wounded in terrorist assaults perpetrated in the international arena and 81 were kidnapped or hijacked. These figures mark a decrease in the categories of victims killed and wounded compared with the previous year's rates. In 1988, 626 people were killed, 1,688 were wounded and 80 were kidnapped in international terrorist acts.

Nine nationalities, along with the general category of international institutions, were involved in 78 percent of all incidents with victims. As in the previous year, American and Pakistani citizens were the most common target for incidents that resulted in casualties. Figures relating to American victims were marked by an increase compared with 1988 (21.2 percent compared to 17.4 percent), while the relative share of Pakistani nationals among those victimized in terrorist assaults decreased in 1989 compared to 1988 (10.6 percent compared to 17.4 percent). Notably, American citizens formed the target for attacks perpetrated worldwide by diverse unrelated elements, while Pakistanis were by and large the victims of a concerted bombing campaign carried out on Pakistani soil, allegedly by Afghan state agents.

A look at larger categories of victims by their affiliation to political blocs reveals no change vis-a-vis previous years' trends. Thus, nationals of countries affiliated with NATO were victimized in 48.1 percent of the 131 incidents that resulted in casualties--a slight increase compared with the 45.8 percent recorded in 1988. Indeed, western states remained the preferred targets for incidents that resulted in victims, while figures for Arab League victims (10.4 percent in 1989) marked a decrease compared with the 1988 rate (13.2 percent). Warsaw Pact nationals accounted for only three incidents that involved victims, comprising 2.2 percent of this category.

For details see Tables 10 and 11 and Figure 4 in Chapter 3.


### The Perpetrators

All told, 55 terrorist organizations were involved in international terrorist activity in 1989. Of these, six groups of diverse nationalities were responsible for 32 percent of the total number of incidents. Also notable was the activity of Chilean, Colombian and Turkish elements whose organizational affiliation was unclear; and the activity of Afghan state agents (2.9 percent). In general, state involvement in international terrorism declined compared to the previous year: in 1988, incidents attributed to Afghan state agents comprised 6.7 percent of the world total; in 1987, 5.3 percent.

Turning to the geographical distribution of perpetrators, Middle Eastern terrorists accounted for 8.9 percent of total incidents perpetrated by the "majors." This figure breaks down to 27 incidents (6.7 percent) perpetrated by Hizballah, and nine (2.2 percent) attributed to unidentified Turkish elements. The relative share of Middle Eastern perpetrators in all international terrorism in 1989 maintains the decline noted over the past two years, compared with 1985 and 1986, when they were responsible for 30 and 25 percent,

13

respectively, of total incidents. Also notable in 1989 was the absence of Palestinian elements and Iranian state-agents in the list of "majors."

Middle Eastern international terrorism is discussed comprehensively in Chapters 4, 5 and 6 of this volume.

Latin American elements were responsible for 17.4 percent of international terrorism in 1989-- corresponding with their relative share recorded in 1988. As in recent years, the two foci of international activity in the region were Colombia and Peru. The Colombian Ejercito de Liberacion Nacional (ELN) alone was responsible for some 8.6 percent of the world total. Most of the recorded attacks, however, were part of an ongoing bombing campaign against an internationally operated fuel pipeline, and were aimed primarily at causing property damage. The Peruvian Sendero Luminoso (SL) was held responsible for 2.9 percent of the incidents carried out in the international sphere. The activity of these Latin American groups, unlike Middle Eastern terrorist elements, was confined to the boundaries of their countries.

The Basque Euskadi Ta Askatasuna (ETA) has been the most active Western European organization included in the list of major perpetrating groups for several years. In 1989 it was joined by the Provisional Irish Republican Army (PIRA), which initiated a campaign against British soldiers in Western Europe. ETA carried out 23 international attacks, or 5.6 percent of the total number of terrorist incidents in the international arena in 1989. Attacks perpetrated by ETA mainly targeted French objectives; this has been the trend since the summer of 1984, and constitutes a response to measures taken by France, alone and in cooperation with Spain, against ETA. Ten attacks carried out in 1989 in the international sphere were attributed to PIRA, comprising 2.5 percent of the world total.

In Asia, the most active elements in the international arena were the New People's Army (NPA) in the Philippines, South Korean Leftists--both of whom

14

targeted mainly American objectives--and Afghan state agents.

In Africa, the Resistancia Nacional Mozambicane (MNR, also known as Renamo) conducted a cross-border campaign into Zimbabwe and Zambia. In 1989 it was held responsible for 16 attacks, comprising 4 percent of the total of world international terrorism.

For details see Tables 7, 8, 9 and 10 and Figure 3 in Chapter 3.


### State Terrorism vs. Independent Groups

In 1989, only 23 incidents--comprising 5.6 percent of total international attacks--were perpetrated by the agents of sovereign states. This relative share marks a decrease compared with the past two years.

State international terrorism differed from non-state international terrorism in the choice of target. The Afghani-directed bombing campaign against civilian targets in Pakistan was a dominant factor in making the random public the preferred target for international state terrorism. Political adversaries formed the second most preferred target for state terrorism, followed by diplomatic objectives--including embassies, consulates and diplomats.

The limited range of operational tactics employed by state agents in 1989 contrasted sharply with the diverse methods practiced by non-state terrorist elements. Thus, state terrorist tactics comprised primarily bombing (17 incidents); only three armed assaults by state agents were recorded, followed by two specific threats and one kidnapping.

One of those threats gave cause to dramatic international developments and public concern, involving the United Kingdom as well as the interests of several other countries. The death sentence issued by the late leader of Iran, Ayatollah Khomeini, against the British author Salman Rushdie appeared temporarily to halt the process

15

of rehabilitating Iran's links with the western world. The threat also generated several international terrorist incidents and a world-wide spate of minor attacks of domestic origin.

For details see Tables 5 and 6 in Chapter 3. Additional attacks perpetrated by organizations directly associated with states are included in the statistics referring to perpetrating groups.

# 3. STATISTICAL TABLES

CONTENTS Page

I.   International Terrorism in 1989: General
     Features

Figure  1.  distribution of incidents  by modus
            operandi                                    19
 Table  1.  distribution of incidents by site of
            incident: country                          20
 Table  2.  distribution of incidents by site of
            incident: region                           21
 Table  3.  modus operandi by site of incident:
            region                                     22
Figure  2.  distribution of incidents according
            to site of incident and nationality
            of target                                  23
 Table  4.  distribution of incidents by nature
            of target                                  24


II.  State vs. Non-State International Terrorism
     in 1989

 Table  5.  state terrorism vs. non-state
            terrorism, by modus operandi               25
 Table  6.  state terrorism vs. non-state
            terrorism, by nature of target             26


III. Major Perpetrating Groups

Figure  3.  distribution of incidents by major
            perpetrating group                         27
 Table  7.  major perpetrating groups by site
            of incident: region                        28
 Table  8.  major perpetrating groups by modus
            operandi                                   29

Table 9.  major perpetrating groups by aim of
          incident                                    30
Table 10. number of incidents in which victims
          were killed by major perpetrating
          groups                                      31


IV.  Victims of International Terrorism in 1989

Figure 4.  distribution of incidents by
           affiliation of victims to political
           blocs                                      32
Table 11.  distribution of incidents by
           nationality of target victims              33


V.   Attacks against Civil Aviation in 1989

Table 12.  distribution of aviation targets by
           modus operandi                             34
Table 13.  distribution of attacks against
           aviation objectives by nationality
           of target                                  35

Figure 1

# Distribution of Incidents *
# by Modus Operandi

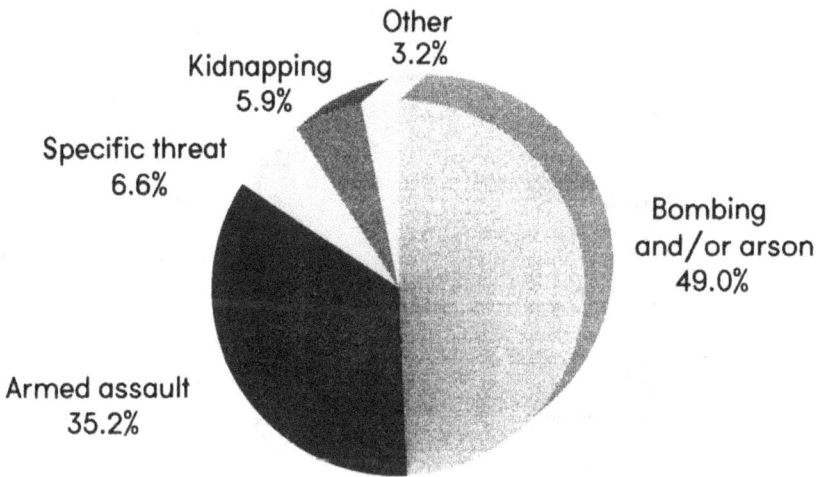

Other 3.2%

Kidnapping 5.9%

Specific threat 6.6%

Bombing and/or arson 49.0%

Armed assault 35.2%

* Total number of incidents – 406

**Table 1**

**DISTRIBUTION OF INCIDENTS,
BY SITE OF INCIDENT: COUNTRY
(countries in which ten
or more incidents took place)**

| Country | Number of Incidents | Percentage of Total |
|---|---|---|
| Colombia | 51 | 12.6 |
| Chile | 27 | 6.6 |
| Peru | 24 | 5.9 |
| Pakistan | 23 | 5.6 |
| Lebanon | 22 | 5.4 |
| Spain | 20 | 4.9 |
| Philippines | 17 | 4.2 |
| South Korea | 16 | 3.9 |
| Federal Republic of Germany | 13 | 3.2 |
| Turkey | 13 | 3.2 |
| El Salvador | 11 | 2.8 |
| Honduras | 11 | 2.8 |
| Other | 158 | 38.9 |
| Total | 406 | 100.0 |

**Table 2**

**DISTRIBUTION OF INCIDENTS,**

**BY SITE OF INCIDENT: REGION**

| Region | Number of Incidents | Percentage of Total |
|--------|--------------------|--------------------|
| AMERICA | | |
| North | 4 | 1.0 |
| Central | 33 | 8.1 |
| South | 117 | 28.9 |
| CARIBBEAN | 8 | 2.0 |
| EUROPE | | |
| Eastern | 3 | 0.7 |
| Western | 80 | 19.7 |
| AFRICA | | |
| North | 9 | 2.2 |
| Subsaharan | 25 | 6.2 |
| South | 4 | 1.0 |
| MIDDLE EAST | 48 | 11.8 |
| ASIA | | |
| South | 27 | 6.6 |
| Southeast | 5 | 1.2 |
| FAR EAST | 41 | 10.1 |
| OCEANIA | 2 | 0.5 |
| Total | 406 | 100 |

Table 3

MODUS OPERANDI*. BY SITE OF INCIDENT: REGION

| Region | Armed Assault | Barricade Hostage | Bombing or Arson | Hijacking | Kidnapping | Letter Bomb | Sabotage | Specific Threat | Poisoning | Unknown | Total |
|---|---|---|---|---|---|---|---|---|---|---|---|
| **AMERICA** | | | | | | | | | | | |
| North | 1 | - | 1 | 1 | - | - | - | - | 1 | - | 4 |
| Central | 18 | 3 | 9 | - | 2 | - | - | - | - | 1 | 33 |
| South | 36 | - | 67 | - | 12 | - | - | 2 | - | - | 117 |
| **CARIBBEAN** | 5 | - | 3 | - | - | - | - | - | - | - | 8 |
| **EUROPE** | | | | | | | | | | | |
| Eastern | - | - | 3 | - | - | - | - | - | - | - | 3 |
| Western | 18 | 2 | 54 | - | - | 1 | 1 | 4 | - | - | 80 |
| **AFRICA** | | | | | | | | | | | |
| North | 7 | - | 2 | - | - | - | - | - | - | - | 9 |
| Subsaharan | 19 | - | 4 | 1 | 1 | - | - | - | - | - | 25 |
| South | 1 | - | 3 | - | - | - | - | - | - | - | 4 |
| **MIDDLE EAST** | 10 | - | 23 | - | 5 | - | 1 | 9 | - | - | 48 |
| **ASIA** | 28 | - | 29 | - | 4 | - | - | 12 | - | - | 73 |
| **OCEANIA** | - | - | 1 | - | - | - | 1 | - | - | - | 2 |
| Total | 143 | 5 | 199 | 2 | 24 | 1 | 3 | 27 | 1 | 1 | 406 |

* Incomplete/thwarted incidents are classified according to their intended modus operandi.

22

Figure 2

# Distribution of Incidents *
# according to Site of Incident
# and Nationality of Target

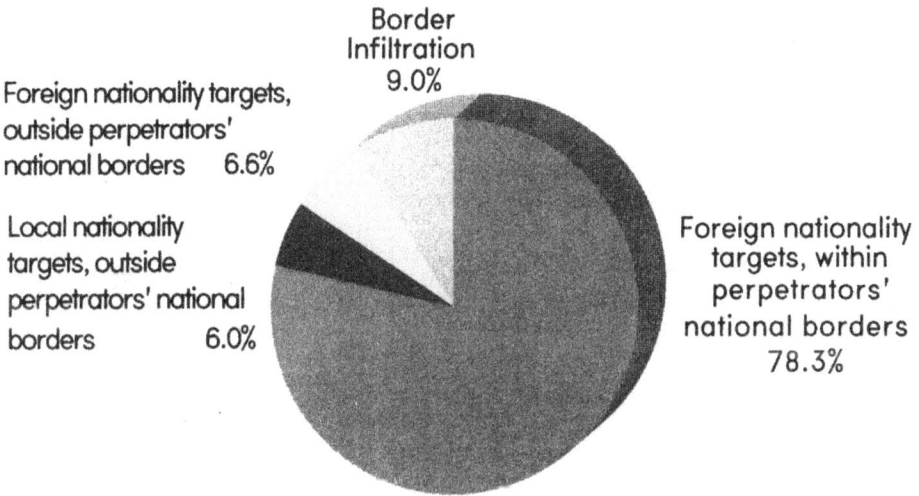

Border
Infiltration
9.0%

Foreign nationality targets,
outside perpetrators'
national borders     6.6%

Local nationality
targets, outside
perpetrators' national
borders          6.0%

Foreign nationality
targets, within
perpetrators'
national borders
78.3%

* Total number of incidents – 378;
    threat and letter bomb incidents not included.

**Table 4**

# DISTRIBUTION OF INCIDENTS*,
# BY NATURE OF TARGET
# (persons/facilities)

| Nature of Target | Number of Incidents |
|---|---|
| Political & Adversary** | 171 |
| Random public | 92 |
| Economic | 130 |
| Diplomatic*** | 101 |
| Unclear | 4 |

* Some of the incidents include more than one type of target.

** Government officials and facilities, political rivals.

*** Embassies, Diplomats, Consulates.

**Table 5**

## STATE TERRORISM VS. NON-STATE TERRORISM, BY MODUS OPERANDI

| Modus operandi* | Incidents of terrorism | | | |
| --- | --- | --- | --- | --- |
| | Non-State Terrorism | State Terrorism | Unclear | Total |
| Armed assault | 135 | 3 | 5 | 143 |
| Barricade-hostage | 5 | - | - | 5 |
| Bombing or arson | 177 | 17 | 5 | 199 |
| Hijacking | 1 | - | 1 | 2 |
| Kidnapping | 23 | 1 | - | 24 |
| Letter bomb | 1 | - | - | 1 |
| Sabotage | 3 | - | - | 3 |
| Specific threat | 25 | 2 | - | 27 |
| Poisoning | - | - | 1 | 1 |
| Unknown | 1 | - | - | 1 |
| Total | 371 | 23 | 12 | 406 |
| Percentage of Total | 91.4 | 5.6 | 3.0 | 100 |

* Incomplete/thwarted incidents are classified according to their intended modus operandi.

**Table 6**

## STATE TERRORISM VS. NON-STATE TERRORISM, BY NATURE OF TARGET*

| Nature of target | Incidents of terrorism | | | |
| --- | --- | --- | --- | --- |
| | Non-State Terrorism | State Terrorism | Unclear | Total |
| Political and adversary** | 160 | 9 | 2 | 171 |
| Random Public | 70 | 16 | 6 | 92 |
| Economic | 123 | 4 | 3 | 130 |
| Diplomatic*** | 93 | 1 | 7 | 101 |
| Unclear | 4 | - | - | 4 |

* Some of the incidents include more than one type of target.

** Government officials and facilities, political rivals.

*** Embassies, diplomats, consulates.

26

Figure   3

# Distribution of Incidents *
# by Major Perpetrating Group

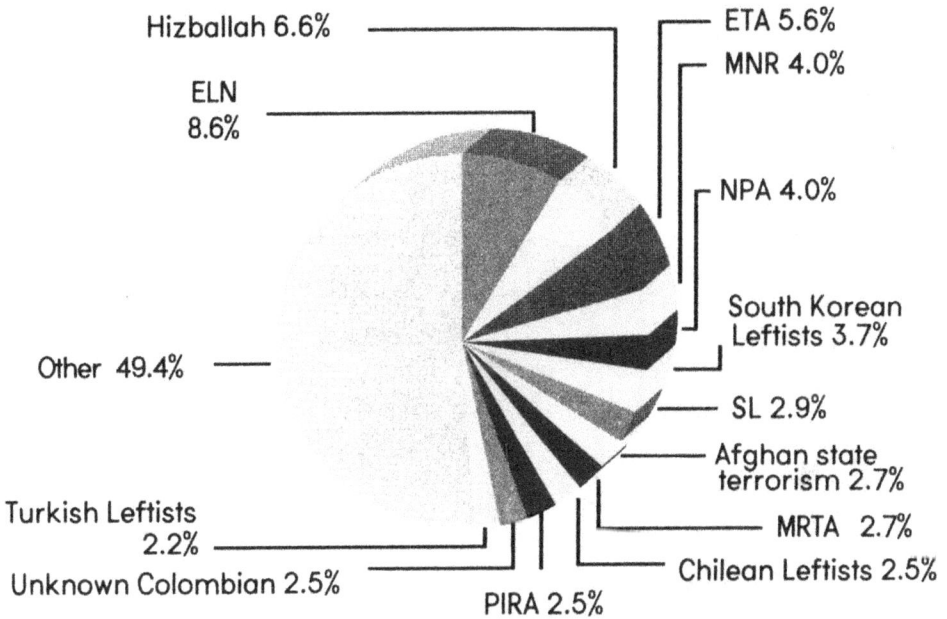

Hizballah 6.6%

ELN 8.6%

ETA 5.6%

MNR 4.0%

NPA 4.0%

South Korean Leftists 3.7%

Other 49.4%

SL 2.9%

Afghan state terrorism 2.7%

MRTA 2.7%

Turkish Leftists 2.2%

Unknown Colombian 2.5%

Chilean Leftists 2.5%

PIRA 2.5%

* Total number of incidents – 406

Table 7

MAJOR PERPETRATING GROUPS, BY SITE OF INCIDENT: REGION

| Region | ELN | Hizb-Allah | ETA | MNR | NPA | South Korean Leftists | SL | Afghan State Terrorism | MRTA | Chilean Leftists | PIRA | Unknown Colombian | Turkish Leftists | Other | Total |
|---|---|---|---|---|---|---|---|---|---|---|---|---|---|---|---|
| AMERICA | | | | | | | | | | | | | | | |
| North | - | 1 | - | - | - | - | - | - | - | - | - | - | - | 3 | 4 |
| Central | - | - | - | - | - | - | - | - | - | - | - | - | - | 33 | 33 |
| South | 35 | - | - | - | - | - | 12 | - | 11 | 10 | - | 10 | - | 39 | 117 |
| CARRIBEAN | - | - | - | - | - | - | - | - | - | - | - | - | - | 8 | 8 |
| EUROPE | | | | | | | | | | | | | | | |
| Eastern | - | - | - | - | - | - | - | - | - | - | - | - | - | 3 | 3 |
| Western | - | 5 | 23 | - | - | - | - | - | - | - | 10 | - | - | 42 | 80 |
| AFRICA | | | | | | | | | | | | | | | |
| North | - | - | - | - | - | - | - | - | - | - | - | - | - | 9 | 9 |
| Subsaharan | - | 1 | - | 16 | - | - | - | - | - | - | - | - | - | 8 | 25 |
| South | - | - | - | - | - | - | - | - | - | - | - | - | - | 4 | 4 |
| MIDDLE EAST | - | 20 | - | - | - | - | - | - | - | - | - | - | 9 | 19 | 48 |
| ASIA | - | - | - | - | 16 | 15 | - | 11 | - | - | - | - | - | 30 | 73 |
| OCEANIA | - | - | - | - | - | - | - | - | - | - | - | - | - | 2 | 2 |
| Total | 35 | 27 | 23 | 16 | 16 | 15 | 12 | 11 | 11 | 10 | 10 | 10 | 9 | 201 | 406 |

Table 8

# MAJOR PERPETRATING GROUPS, BY MODUS OPERANDI

| Aim of Incident | ELN | Hizb-Allah | ETA | MNR | NPA | South Korean Leftists | SL | Afghan State Terrorism | MRTA | Chilean Leftists | PIRA | Unknown Colombian | Turkish Leftists | Other | Total |
|---|---|---|---|---|---|---|---|---|---|---|---|---|---|---|---|
| Armed assault | 5 | 5 | 1 | 14 | 7 | 14 | 6 | - | 4 | 3 | 3 | 4 | 2 | 75 | 143 |
| Barricade-hostage | - | - | - | - | - | - | - | - | 5 | - | - | - | - | 5 | 5 |
| Bombing or arson | 24 | 11 | 22 | 1 | 4 | 1 | 4 | 11 | 6 | 7 | 7 | 4 | 7 | 90 | 199 |
| Hijacking | - | - | - | - | - | - | - | - | - | - | - | - | - | 2 | 2 |
| Kidnapping | 6 | 3 | - | 1 | 1 | - | 2 | - | - | - | - | 2 | - | 9 | 24 |
| Letter bomb | - | - | - | - | - | - | - | - | - | - | - | - | - | 1 | 1 |
| Poisoning | - | - | - | - | - | - | - | - | - | - | - | - | - | 1 | 1 |
| Sabotage | - | - | - | - | - | - | - | - | - | - | - | - | - | 3 | 3 |
| Specific threat | - | 8 | - | - | 4 | - | - | - | 1 | - | - | - | - | 14 | 27 |
| Unknown | - | - | - | - | - | - | - | - | - | - | - | - | - | 1 | 1 |
| Total | 35 | 27 | 23 | 16 | 16 | 15 | 12 | 11 | 11 | 10 | 10 | 10 | 9 | 201 | 406 |

*Incomplete/thwarted incidents are classified according to their intended modus operandi.

# Table 9

## MAJOR PERPETRATING GROUPS, BY AIM OF INCIDENT

| Aim of Incident | ELN | Hizb-Allah | ETA | MNR | NPA | South Korean Leftists | SL | Afghan State Terrorism | MRTA | Chilean Leftists | PIRA | Unknown Colombian | Turkish Leftists | Other | Total |
|---|---|---|---|---|---|---|---|---|---|---|---|---|---|---|---|
| Assassination | - | 5 | - | - | 2 | - | 2 | - | - | - | - | - | - | 20 | 29 |
| Extortion | 4 | 2 | - | 1 | 1 | - | 1 | - | - | - | - | - | - | 9 | 18 |
| Killing & property damage | 1 | 4 | 4 | 1 | 4 | 7 | - | 6 | 4 | 4 | 2 | 3 | 2 | 50 | 92 |
| Property damage alone | 15 | 2 | 19 | - | 3 | 8 | 4 | - | 3 | 6 | - | 5 | 7 | 74 | 146 |
| Random killing | 1 | 6 | - | 14 | 2 | - | 4 | 5 | 1 | - | 8 | - | - | 15 | 56 |
| Other* | 14 | 8 | - | - | 4 | - | 1 | - | 3 | - | - | 2 | - | 33 | 65 |
| Total | 35 | 27 | 23 | 16 | 16 | 15 | 12 | 11 | 11 | 10 | 10 | 10 | 9 | 201 | 406 |

*including threat, propaganda, protest and robbery.

30

**Table  10**


**NUMBER  OF  INCIDENTS  IN  WHICH
VICTIMS  WERE  KILLED,  BY  MAJOR
PERPETRATING  GROUPS**

| Perpet-<br>rating<br>Group | No<br>Deaths | Incidents<br>with Deaths | Number of<br>Deaths<br>Unknown | Total |
|---|---|---|---|---|
| ELN | 31 | 2 | 2 | 35 |
| Hizballah | 17 | 10 | - | 27 |
| ETA | 23 | - | - | 23 |
| MNR | 1 | 15 | - | 16 |
| NPA | 12 | 4 | - | 16 |
| South Korean | | | | |
| Leftists | 13 | 2 | - | 15 |
| SL | 7 | 5 | - | 12 |
| Afghan State | | | | |
| Terrorism | 3 | 8 | - | 11 |
| MRTA | 10 | 1 | - | 11 |
| Chilean | | | | |
| Leftists | 7 | 3 | - | 10 |
| PIRA | 7 | 3 | - | 10 |
| Unknown | | | | |
| Colombian | 7 | 3 | - | 10 |
| Turkish | | | | |
| Leftists | 9 | - | - | 9 |
| Other | 150 | 25 | 26 | 201 |
| Total | 297 | 81 | 28 | 406 |

Figure 4

# Distribution of Incidents *
# by Affiliation of Victims **
# to Political Blocs

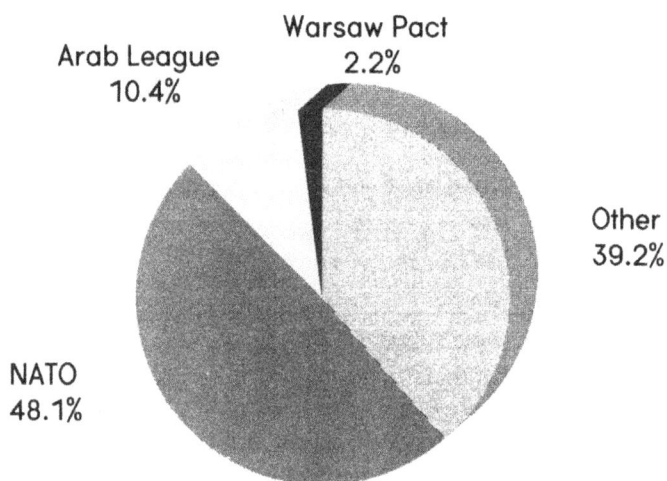

Warsaw Pact
2.2%

Arab League
10.4%

Other
39.2%

NATO
48.1%

\* The total number of incidents with victims was 131; some of the incidents involved victims of more than one political affiliation.

\*\* Victims include killed, wounded & kidnapped (whether or not released by captors).

**Table 11**

## DISTRIBUTION OF INCIDENTS, BY NATIONALITY OF TARGET VICTIMS

| Nationality of Target Victims* | Number of Incidents** | Percentage of Total Incidents with Victims |
|---|---|---|
| USA | 28 | 21.2 |
| Pakistan | 14 | 10.6 |
| United Kingdom | 13 | 9.9 |
| International Organizations | 9 | 6.8 |
| Italy | 8 | 6.1 |
| Saudi Arabia | 8 | 6.1 |
| Federal Republic of Germany | 6 | 4.5 |
| Spain | 6 | 4.5 |
| Zimbabwe | 6 | 4.5 |
| France | 5 | 3.8 |
| Other countries | 29 | 22.0 |
| Total | 132 | 100 |

*Comprises only countries that were the target
of 5 or more attacks. Victims include killed,
wounded and kidnapped (whether of not released
by captors).

**The total number of incidents with victims was 131;
-some of the incidents involved target-victims
of more than one nationality.

**Table 12**

# DISTRIBUTION OF AVIATION

# TARGETS BY MODUS OPERANDI

| Modus Operandi* | Airliner | Airline Office | Airport | Total |
|---|---|---|---|---|
| Armed assault | 1 | - | - | 1 |
| Bombing and arson | 4 | - | - | 4 |
| Hijacking | - | - | - | - |
| Sabotage | - | - | - | - |
| Specific threat | 1 | - | - | 1 |
| Total | 6 | - | - | 6 |

\* Incomplete/thwarted incidents are classified according to their intended modus operandi.

**Table 13**

## DISTRIBUTION OF ATTACKS AGAINST AVIATION OBJECTIVES, BY NATIONALITY OF TARGET

| Nationality of target | Target | | | |
|---|---|---|---|---|
| | Airliner | Airline Office | Airport | Total |
| France | 2 | - | - | 2 |
| Colombia | 1 | - | - | 1 |
| Saudi Arabia | 1 | - | - | 1 |
| United Kingdom | 1 | - | - | 1 |
| USA | 1 | - | - | 1 |
| Total | 6 | - | - | 6 |

* Incomplete/thwarted incidents are classified according to their intended modus operandi.

# 4. SHI'ITE INTERNATIONAL TERRORISM

Since the advent to power of Ayatollah Khomeini in Iran in February 1979, terrorism has been employed as a tool of foreign and interior policy by revolutionary Iran. The phenomenon gained impetus in late 1982, when Hizballah cells began to operate in Lebanon and in the international arena, and Shi'ite terrorism became one of the most prominent expressions of international terrorism.

For the purposes of this survey, Shi'ite terrorism refers to incidents linked to Shi'ite fundamentalist groups that are ideologically affiliated with and materially supported by the Islamic Republic of Iran. International Shi'ite incidents encompass all such incidents involving the interests of more than one country.

A variety of tactics have come to be associated with Iranian-sponsored international terrorism. The most spectacular ones include suicide car bombings and kidnappings of foreign nationals in Lebanon, as well as hijackings of civil airliners. Throughout the period from 1982 until mid-1990, Shi'ite organizations in Lebanon were involved in the abduction of 69 foreign citizens of various nationalities. Shi'ite terrorists were involved in at least 13 actual and attempted international incidents of hijacking (approximately 20 percent of the total of international airliner hijackings in the 1980s). In most cases, both hijackings and abductions developed into prolonged episodes involving many countries and generating international political ramifications.

Diverse states were thus confronted with complex political and diplomatic challenges associated with Shi'ite terrorism. The challenges were directly related to the fact that another sovereign state, seeking to advance its own interests, was the initiator of the terrorist attacks and the active supporter of their perpetrators. Furthermore, the high lethality of some

36

of the acts, and the systematic employment of extortionist tactics--skyjacking and kidnapping-- accentuated the dilemmas posed to decisionmakers in the targeted countries. They had to cope with intense public pressure to safeguard the victims, yet avoid surrendering to the terrorists' demands. In many cases a military option was not available. Indeed, rescue attempts as well as military retaliatory acts were often too risky, both in terms of operational complications and political considerations.

The volume of Shi'ite international terrorism was subject to changes throughout the past decade. Looking at attacks perpetrated by Iranian state agents, Hizballah, Amal, and groups in the Persian Gulf, we note that during the first years following the revolution in Iran, only a few international incidents were recorded. Between 1983 and 1985, following the establishment of Hizballah in Lebanon, Shi'ite elements were involved in 34-41 incidents per year. In 1986-1987, rates of Shi'ite terrorism mounted to 65-66 incidents a year, and constituted 17 percent of the total of international terrorist incidents recorded around the globe in 1987. Since 1988, there has been a marked decrease in the volume of Shi'ite international terrorism, to only 36-40 incidents per year.

Yet Shi'ite international terrorism has not lost its saliency; Iran has continued to play an active role in ongoing affairs such as the hostage crisis in Lebanon, and has provided the inspiration for fresh waves of attacks. The existence of a Shi'ite international terrorist infrastructure, coupled with the enhancement of ties between Tehran and radical Palestinian terrorist elements, presents a potential for more Shi'ite terrorist attacks to be carried out on the international scene in the foreseeable future.

### The Main Actors

A variety of Shi'ite elements have been involved in terrorist activity in the international sphere. In addition to Iranian nationals--usually directed by

37

diplomatic missions abroad--Shi'ite militants from Lebanon, Kuwait, Iraq, Saudi Arabia and Bahrain have been responsible for a considerable share of the attacks.

The different Shi'ite radical groups, although inspired and often directed by Iran, nevertheless represent a variety of interests and motives. "Iran's Revolution reinforced a general phenomenon of Shi'ite political activism. The characteristics of such activism varied from community to community, mediated as it was by local economic and cultural traditions."[1] In spite of the differences, they are all included within a single framework of Shi'ite international terrorism because their activity in the international arena has been, to a large extent, inspired by Iran and aimed at advancing its interests. In many cases it is impossible to trace the origin of the perpetrating group and the extent of Iranian involvement, and therefore difficult to identify some groups as local or foreign elements.

Advancing the ideological and strategic goal of exporting the Islamic Revolution has been a dominant component of Iranian foreign policy. The determination to spread revolutionary fundamentalism formed the backdrop, for example, for an Iranian-sponsored coup attempt in Bahrain in 1981, and for the convening in Tehran in 1982 of a meeting attended by terrorist elements from Middle Eastern and Islamic states.

The most demonstrative expression of Iran's revolutionary drive outside its borders has been its active involvement with **Hizballah** (the Party of God) in Lebanon since 1982. The extent of this involvement has varied according to the specific objectives of operations, as well as the nature of links and degree of dependence on Tehran of the various factions within the movement. Iranian agents have probably not been involved in every detail of operations taking place on the Lebanese domestic scene. Yet attacks of international significance have apparently been coordinated, and in many instances directed, by Iranian political cadres in Tehran and diplomatic representatives in Damascus, Beirut and other capitals.

Iran's involvement in terrorist acts carried out by Shi'ite elements was clearly manifested during the hijackings of civil airliners of western and Gulf airlines. It even went so far as to supply the hijackers of two Kuwaiti planes with weapons and additional logistical assistance after the hijacked planes had landed on its territory: in December 1984 it provided the hijackers with a safe getaway after faking a military raid to rescue the passengers, in which none of the terrorists was hurt; in another incident which began on April 5, 1988, additional terrorists joined the hijackers during a stopover of the commandeered plane at Mashad airport in Iran.[2]

Critical factors that evidently facilitated the promotion of Iranian interests in Lebanon through the activity of a local organization were the disintegration of the latter country's political system as well as the consent, and at times active support, of Syria. Damascus, whose armed forces have long controlled parts of Lebanon, has always addressed the Iranian involvement there within the context of its own interests in the region. These are related mainly to Syria's strategic stance vis-a-vis the Arab-Israel conflict, Syrian-Iranian mutual enmity toward Iraq, and Syria's relationship with western states.

Damascus has been allowing Iranian Revolutionary Guards to cross into Lebanon from Syria's territory since 1982, and has been actively supporting Hizballah's fight against Israel.[3] Sheikh Muhammad Hussein Fadlallah, the spiritual leader of Hizballah, maintains that there is a "strategic understanding" between Syria and his movement concerning the "struggle against Israel and Imperialism," and confirms that Syria has facilitated arms transfers to the Islamic Resistance in Lebanon.[4]

Syrian military intelligence was involved in Hizballah's attacks against western objectives in Lebanon at the beginning of the '80s, including the lethal bombing attacks against French and American troops in Beirut in 1983.[5] The deployment of Syrian troops in the Biq'a Valley, as well as in the western and southern suburbs of Beirut--the areas where Hizballah operates--make it an accomplice in the detention of foreign hostages. Since 1986, Syria has emphasized the key role it must play in any attempt to solve the problem of the foreign hostages, in line with its efforts to improve its own image in the West. "We played an important role to help in the release of a number of foreign hostages in Lebanon...and we believe this role must continue,"[6] noted Syrian Foreign Minister Farouq al-Shara in September 1989. In any event, Syria's involvement with pro-Iranian militancy in Lebanon has always been conditioned upon Damascus' determination to keep developments under its control. Accordingly, it did not hesitate to curb the activity of Iran and Hizballah in Lebanon when it found this necessary, principally by assisting Hizballah's rival, Amal.

Inside Iran, the status of officials linked with Hizballah has changed over time due to the dynamics of the internal power struggle among rival factions within the regime. Intra-organizational frictions among leaders of Hizballah have also affected its relations with Iran. In addition, the interests of Hizballah have not always coincided with those of its patron, but rather have involved considerations relating to local developments in Lebanon. Thus attempts made by the Iranian regime following Khomeini's death to tighten links with the other Lebanese Shi'ite movement, Amal, apparently contradicted Hizballah's interests, as the latter was itself engaged in an ongoing competition with Amal over dominance of the Shi'ite community in the country.

The **Amal** militia was founded in 1975, in an attempt to ensure adequate representation for the Shi'ite population in Lebanon. Unlike Hizballah, it seeks to achieve its goal within the bounds of the existing Lebanese political system. The militia, led by Nabih Berri, is supported by Syria both logistically and politically. Between 1983-1986 Amal was involved in a series of attacks against Libyan objectives in Lebanon and Western Europe. The assaults were carried out in retaliation for the disappearance of its founder, Imam Musa Sadr, in Libya in 1978. Gradually, these attacks expanded in dimension and generated greater international ramifications. Some of the perpetrators of planned attacks were captured by authorities in Spain, Cyprus and the US; these arrests triggered further attacks against these countries' interests in order to obtain the detainees' release. Thus the involvement of Amal in international terrorism has generally not been directed at furthering the interests of a foreign power in the same way that Hizballah has been acting, and has rather been linked with the organization's own specific needs.

Other Shi'ite organizations closely aligned with Iran and involved in international terrorism included primarily Iraqi groups acting from Iranian territory, and terrorist cells in Kuwait and Saudi Arabia. The Iraqi **Dawa** (The Call) was the major suspect in a series of explosions in Kuwait in December 1983, an assassination attempt against the Emir of Kuwait on May 25, 1985, and several acts against Iraqi and Kuwaiti targets, including two incidents of hijacking of civil airliners. The Iraqi **Amal al-Islami** (Islamic Action) and the Iraqi **Mojahiddin** were also held responsible for hijacking incidents, including that of a French airliner on August 27, 1983.

In Saudi Arabia, local Shi'ite terrorists as well as Shi'ite militants originating from Kuwait and other Gulf states were convicted and executed for perpetrating terrorist attacks in the country at Iran's behest during 1988-89. A pro-Iranian group claimed responsibility for an attack against a petrochemical plant in Saudi Arabia in April 1988.

Iran has encouraged, provided logistical support for, and actively directed militant Shi'ite elements operating in Persian Gulf states. Some activities have apparently been coordinated through the apparatus of Hizballah in Lebanon. Hizballah has repeatedly demanded the release of Shi'ite terrorists imprisoned in Kuwait and Saudi Arabia. In retaliation for the execution of Shi'ite terrorists in Saudi Arabia, Hizballah teams resorted to a worldwide campaign against Saudi objectives. In fact, responsibility for many assaults perpetrated in the Gulf region has been claimed in Beirut.

Still, Shi'ite terrorism in Gulf states has usually been perpetrated by ad hoc groups, and remained rather limited in scope and volume. "The fundamentalist movements failed to establish themselves as broadly based guerrilla organizations [in the Gulf],"[7] and in effect lacked the massive popular support considered critical for establishing organizational power. This state of affairs has been traced to two major situational factors. First, support for Iran on the part of the different Shi'ite communities never developed into a popular and organized movement because of socio-political conditions. In addition, governments in Gulf states have conducted a successful carrot-and-stick approach, granting their Shi'ite populace economic incentives while curbing manifestations of opposition. Some of them have expelled Iranians and their local supporters, and have executed convicted terrorists.[8]

### Iranian Terrorism as a Foreign Policy Tool

What kind of political goals and interests has Iran been trying to advance through the employment of terrorism?

At the domestic level, one of the most important tasks of the revolutionary regime in Tehran has been the consolidation and stabilization of the revolution. The spillover of this policy into the international arena was initially reflected in threats against all countries that had supported the Shah, including western and moderate Arab states. At a later stage Iran directed a series of assassinations of opposition figures living in exile abroad. Most of the attacks (77 percent of the total) took place in Western Europe, where many opponents found refuge. (Some of the attacks were excluded from the count of terrorist incidents because they targeted anti-Iranian terrorist elements and were considered part of Iran's own counterterrorism drive.) The asylum provided by France to Khomeini's opponents-- Bani Sadr, Masoud Rajavi, Shapur Bakhtiar and others--

42

has in effect become a focus of controversy between the
two countries.


## Shi'ite Terrorism against Persian Gulf States

From the perspective of regional strategic interests,
Iran has employed terrorist methods as part of its quest
for hegemony in the Persian Gulf.   One primary goal
within this context was to isolate Iraq, Iran's enemy in
the Gulf War, by terrorizing its supporters, mainly
Saudi Arabia and Kuwait.  Further, Saudi and Kuwaiti oil
policies have been perceived by Iran as damaging to its
own interests.   Thus terrorist campaigns have been
conducted against the interests of Persian Gulf
countries, targeting oil installations as well as
diplomatic missions.   Iran strongly rejects Saudi
Arabia's ties with the US, its acceptance of an American
military presence in the Gulf, and its general pro-
western attitude.   In addition, Iran's opposition to
Saudi rule over the Islamic Holy Places has resulted in
repeated attempts to disrupt the annual pilgrimage to
Mecca.

The highest rate of attacks against Gulf states was
recorded in 1984, when they formed the target of 43
percent of the total of Shi'ite international attacks.
The considerable anti-Kuwaiti share of the attacks that
year was directly associated with the conviction of 17
Shi'ite terrorists responsible for bombing attacks
against French, American and local targets in Kuwait on
December 12, 1983.  Those attacks were carried out by
Shi'ites inspired by Iran and Hizballah, most of whom
were Iraqi, Iranian and Lebanese nationals; only one was
of Kuwaiti origin.[9]   They belonged to Al Dawa, the
Iranian-sponsored Shi'ite organization.   Since then,
Hizballah in Lebanon has perpetrated intensive
kidnapping campaigns and hijacked civil airliners of
Kuwaiti and other companies in an attempt to gain the
release of the 17 terrorists from Kuwaiti jails and to
prevent implementation of pending death sentences.  By
May 1990 the death sentences had not been implemented:
15 terrorists remained imprisoned; two had completed
their five-year terms.

Several developments in the Persian Gulf in 1987 generated increased violence in the region. Kuwait was targeted in a series of bombing attacks on the eve of the Islamic Summit convened in its capital in January, which was strongly opposed by Iran. Anti-Kuwaiti attacks continued throughout the year against the backdrop of the American reflagging operation for the defense of Kuwaiti oil tankers in the Gulf. Another, unrelated development, with repercussions for Iran's relations with Saudi Arabia, was the death of hundreds of Iranian pilgrims during the annual pilgrimage to Mecca on July 31, 1987. The pilgrims were killed in clashes with Saudi security forces after Iranian demonstrators provoked rioting.

Iran's threats of vengeance materialized in an intensive terrorist campaign against Saudi interests all over the world during 1988-1990. The attacks were also linked to the execution in September 1988 of Shi'ite terrorists in Saudi Arabia, and were possibly authorized by radical elements within the Iranian regime seeking to disrupt concurrent attempts at rapprochement between Riyadh and the government in Tehran.[10] The first stage of the anti-Saudi campaign focused on bombing attacks against Saudi airline offices in Singapore, Malaysia, Japan, Pakistan, FRG and Kuwait. It was followed by a series of assassinations of Saudi diplomats, perpetrated by Iranian state-agents in Turkey, Pakistan, Thailand, Belgium, and Lebanon. Iran was also accused of involvement in a series of bombings that took place in Mecca during the annual Hajj in July 1989.[11] The Mecca bombings, in turn, produced a new catalyst for acts of vengeance against Saudi targets, when their Shi'ite perpetrators were executed by the Saudi authorities. These included an attempt to blow up a Saudi jetliner in midair after take-off from Pakistan, which was thwarted on November 23, 1989.

## Shi'ite Terrorism against Western European States

Iran's fundamental rejection of the western world, and particularly of the United States, has formed the ideological backdrop to assaults against western interests. Yet international terrorism directed by Iran has specifically aimed at advancing concrete political and economic interests.

Since 1983 Western European states, and particularly France, have been frequent targets as well as venues for Shi'ite terrorism. The infrastructure of Shi'ite terrorism in Western Europe has been based mainly on Iran's embassies and diplomatic representatives as well as on Middle Eastern and North African activists living in Europe. The embassies fill a logistical role of supplying operatives with arms and explosives, finances and safe havens. They also form a liaison channel with Tehran, deliver instructions for operations, and engage in the recruitment of new activists among Shi'ite students and immigrants. Links with local terrorist groups have in effect proved of negligible value for state-sponsored militants that enjoy the logistical backing of foreign legations abroad. In any event, allegations concerning ties between Hizballah and Western European organizations have not been corroborated, and lack concrete evidence.[12]

The most spectacular manifestation of Shi'ite terrorist activity against Western European states and the USA beyond their boundaries, has been the abduction of their nationals by Hizballah in Lebanon.[13] The kidnapping of foreign nationals, mainly French and American, was primarily initiated in order to pressure Kuwait into releasing Shi'ite terrorists arrested since the December 1983 bombing attacks in its capital. Yet Iran has long since become the main beneficiary of the prolonged detention, by its surrogates, of hostages in the cellars of densely-populated Shi'ite neighborhoods in Beirut and elsewhere in Lebanon.

The fate of abducted French nationals has been directly linked with the state of bilateral relations between France and Iran. By May 1988 all French nationals among the western hostages had been released, and no new French hostages had been taken by mid-1990. Deals reportedly concluded between Paris and Tehran granted Iran considerable economic, diplomatic and political benefits in return for the release of hostages. Thus the kidnapping of French nationals was a critical factor in persuading France to pay back to Iran a loan made by the late Shah to the French Eurodif uranium enrichment consortium in 1975. Diplomatic relations between the two states improved concurrently, as France also yielded to Iran's demands to expel members of the Iranian exile opposition from Paris. France also reportedly paid ransom to the kidnappers in Lebanon to bring the French part of the hostage affair to an end.[14] The releases were achieved through secret negotiations conducted with Iran and with Hizballah in Lebanon. Mediators included individuals as well as states--primarily Syria and Algeria.

The fate of the French hostages was linked to several additional issues that formed the backdrop for violent activity against French interests. While the involvement of France and the US in Lebanon within the framework of the Multi-National Force (MNF) provoked attacks against their interests in Lebanon and Kuwait during 1983-84, it was the military assistance that France provided to Iraq that generated most of the Iranian-sponsored terrorist attacks against France. Thus attacks against French interests in Lebanon during 1981-1982 were at least partially instigated by France's delivery of 60 Mirage F-1 jets to Iraq in January 1981. The further delivery of French Super Etendard aircraft and Exocet missiles to Iraq in October 1983 brought about additional attacks in France in December of that year.

During February, March and September 1986, Hizballah was involved in concerted attacks on crowded shopping centers and public places in France, as Iran sought to stop French arms sales to Iraq.[15] Indeed, the highest rates of Shi'ite terrorism against Western Europe were recorded that year--54 percent of the total Shi'ite international attacks. Responsibility for the 1986 bombings in Paris was claimed by the Committee for Solidarity with Arab and Middle Eastern Political Prisoners (CSAMPP) on behalf of the Lebanese Armed Revolutionary Factions (LARF). The explicit demand presented by CSAMPP was the release from French jails of three convicted terrorists: George Ibrahim Abdallah, leader of LARF; Anis Naccash, a Fatah member who had led an assassination attempt against the former Iranian prime minister, Shapour Bakhtiar, on July 18, 1980; and Varodjian Garbidjian, a member of the Armenian Secret Army for the Liberation of Armenia (ASALA).

Iran's prominent role in these attacks became evident in mid-1987, following the arrest in Paris of North African and Lebanese members of a Hizballah network, the uncovering of explosives caches, and disclosures concerning the involvement of Iranian Embassy officials in the attacks. Tensions between France and Iran culminated in July 1987 over the case of Wahid Gordji, an employee at the Iranian Embassy in Paris who had taken refuge in the Embassy to avoid being interrogated by French authorities regarding his alleged involvement in the bombing campaigns. The trial of the network members opened in France on January 29, 1990.

The network exposed in France maintained links with other Hizballah cells in Western Europe. Arrests of activists in FRG and Italy in January 1987 foiled plans to attack Jewish, Israeli and American objectives in Western Europe.[16] Muhammad Ali Hamadi, a Hizballah member arrested in FRG for the possession of explosives, had been long sought for his involvement in the 1985 hijacking of TWA flight 847 to Beirut, for which the US was seeking his extradition. His arrest and subsequent trial provoked repeated threats by Shi'ite elements against the FRG, and provided a motive for the kidnapping of West German citizens in Lebanon.

The uncovering of pro-Iranian cells in Western Europe during 1987 apparently was a major blow to the Shi'ite terrorist infrastructure in this part of the world. A relative decrease was subsequently recorded in the volume of Shi'ite incidents recorded in Western Europe during 1988-1989. This was coupled with a shift of terrorist activity toward peripheral arenas such as Asia, the Far East and Africa. Indeed, Shi'ite activists who managed to escape arrest in Europe fled to West Africa,[17] turning this region into a new, albeit remote, departure base for terrorist activity in Western

Europe. Yet this lower profile of activity in Western Europe was evidently only temporary, as indicated by the exposure of a new Shi'ite terrorist network in Spain in November 1989. Large quantities of explosives smuggled from Lebanon to Spanish ports as well as to Cyprus and France were destined for lethal bombing attacks in Western Europe, with France, again, as the primary objective.[18]

The publication in Britain and the US of the novel *The Satanic Verses* provoked Khomeini to issue a death sentence on February 14, 1989 against the author, Salman Rushdie. The 'verdict' created an international furor, particularly in the western world; it was followed by a series of threats and bombing attacks against bookshops and publishing houses. Most of the incidents occurred in the US and in Britain, Italy and France. They were generally minor and non-lethal and were apparently intended to intimidate by causing damage only. A few related attacks against British and American targets occurred in Pakistan. Few suspects were arrested, and it seems likely that these attacks were perpetrated by local Muslims, not necessarily Shi'ites, who were inspired by Tehran's attitude and acted alone or within the framework of ad hoc groups. It appears less probable that the assailants were Middle Eastern nationals sent to the scene by an organized terrorist apparatus or a state. In effect, only one attack was thought to have been perpetrated by a Hizballah team: on March 29, 1989 the Saudi leader of the Muslim community in Belgium and his deputy were assassinated, allegedly because of their "too moderate" reaction to the publication of Rushdie's novel. Still, exploitation of religious zealotry linked to the Rushdie affair in a more organized and systematic manner should not be ruled out within the framework of anti-western terrorist activity in future.

### Shi'ite Terrorism against the United States

Although the US has been a major target for Shi'ite terrorism, few Shi'ite terrorist incidents have actually been perpetrated on American territory. Exceptions include a few attacks on Khomeini's opponents in 1979-1980, and a bombing attack by an improvised explosive charge in 1989 targeting the car of the commander of the US cruiser that had downed an Iranian jetliner over the Persian Gulf the previous year. This pattern is not unique to Shi'ite terrorism. Rather, it is typical of Middle Eastern terrorism as a whole, and is thought to stem from two main factors. One is the strict law-enforcement measures and immigration restrictions implemented by the US; the other reflects political considerations that presumably lead organizations and sponsoring states to refrain from crossing a threshold perceived as too flagrant and, therefore, counterproductive.

The first spectacular terrorist assault against the US took place in 1983 in Lebanon, when a suicide carbomb exploded on April 18 in front of the US Embassy. On October 23 that year, carbombs apparently hit the headquarters of the US Marines and of French paratroops. The attacks, which resulted in 316 casualties, were aimed at driving the Multi-National Force (MNF) out of Lebanon--a process that culminated in February 1984 when the Marines indeed began to leave the country.

The actual involvement of Shi'ite suicides in these attacks was never confirmed. Alternative explanations suggested that the assailants of the French and US headquarters were misled by their despatchers;[19] French sources claimed in 1989 that the French headquarters were not hit by a carbomb but rather by explosive charges that had been planted earlier in the building.[20] In any event, suicide carbombing has since become a preferred tactic of Shi'ite terrorists, primarily in their struggle to force the Israel Defense Forces out of Lebanon. It has also become a model for other militant groups in Lebanon, mainly pro-Syrian Leftist secular elements. These carbomb attacks, involving considerable quantities of explosives, sophisticated devices and a high level of pre-operational intelligence, were carried out with the consent and active involvement of Syria.[21]

The highest rate of Shi'ite terrorism against the US was recorded in 1984, when assaults against American interests constituted 29 percent of total Shi'ite international terrorist incidents. Most of these were abductions of American citizens in Lebanon, aimed at gaining the release of the terrorists that had been arrested in Kuwait in December 1983. During the following years, American citizens, diplomatic staff and officials became frequent targets for kidnapping and skyjacking.

Deliveries of US arms to Iran from August-September 1985 and throughout 1986, within the framework of the Iran-Contra arms-for-hostages deals,[22] apparently led to a decline in Shi'ite terrorism against American targets, evident in 1986. That year assaults against American objectives constituted only 8 percent of the total of Shi'ite international terrorism. The deals were conducted by members of the US National Security Staff, and one of their objectives was to resolve the hostage problem in Lebanon. The Iranian-initiated disclosure of the secret deals, and the halt of the deliveries, were a principal factor in instigating an intense campaign of kidnappings of American and other foreign citizens in Lebanon in January 1987.

In addition to the issue of the Shi'ite detainees held in Kuwait, the systematic use of these extortionist tactics against the US was also aimed at achieving the release of Lebanese Shi'ites detained by Israel. This pattern of extortion from Washington as an indirect means of gaining concessions from its allies has repeatedly been evident throughout the hostage affair in Lebanon, as time and again the kidnappers have issued threats linking the fate of American captives with Israel's policy in Southern Lebanon. This was clearly demonstrated after the IDF's capture of Sheikh Abd al-Karim Obeid, a Hizballah leader, in Lebanon on July 28, 1989. The Israeli action was part of an effort to free three Israeli POWs held by Shi'ite elements in Lebanon since 1986. Hizballah first threatened to kill American hostages unless Israel released the Sheikh, then claimed that it had executed American hostage William Higgins, a Marine officer seconded to the UN who had been kidnapped by Hizballah on February 17, 1988 and accused of espionage. The Israeli step generated tensions between the US and Israel, though it soon became apparent that Higgins had died earlier, and that the Obeid affair was being used as a face-saving opportunity to publicize his death and gain political profits.

The same phenomenon was manifested during the hijacking of an American TWA airliner on June 14, 1985. The hijackers, members of Hizballah and an extremist faction of Amal, demanded the release of Shi'ites imprisoned in Kuwait, Israel and Spain, and called for the cancellation of the Israeli-monitored Southern Lebanon Security Zone. When their demand to refuel the plane was not granted, they murdered an American Navy diver. The episode came to an end after 17 days of negotiations between the US and Amal leader Nabih Berri. Israel later gradually released Shi'ite detainees, although it claimed that the release had no connection with the conclusion of the hijacking incident.

By May 1990 Shi'ite elements were reportedly holding 11 western hostages (Abu-Nidal's Fatah Revolutionary Cells and other organizations were holding several others). Six of the 11 hostages were American nationals who remained in captivity following the release of their compatriots, Robert Polhill and Frank Reed, on April 22 and April 30, 1990, respectively. Those releases, after a three-year deadlock in the American hostage issue, followed reports published since September 1989 and throughout the first months of 1990, alleging that the administration was secretly negotiating with Iran over the fate of the American hostages.[23] All these reports were denied categorically by Washington, which reiterated the official American position that the US would not pay money to Iran as part of an exchange.

On October 23, 1989 Iran's President Hashemi Rafsanjani, in his first news conference since assuming the presidency, offered to help the US obtain the freedom of American hostages. In return, Washington was asked to restore Iranian assets frozen in the US since 1979, and to provide a clear explanation concerning the fate of three Iranian hostages captured by Christian elements in Lebanon in 1982.[24] A US readiness to unfreeze $567 million was reported in November. In May 1990, shortly after the two hostage releases in Lebanon, the US and Iran reached two agreements at the Hague which would eventually produce additional settlement of Iranian financial claims.

The new Iranian attitude demonstrated the complexity of the hostage affair. The newly-elected president of Iran was linking the fate of the American hostages with his efforts to rehabilitate his country after the ceasefire in the Gulf War. Yet the outcome of his policy was also tightly linked with a concurrent power struggle within the ruling elite in Tehran. Internal instability was mirrored in contradictory editorials published in Tehran newspapers concerning the prospects for a solution of the hostage affair. Furthermore, media reports on alleged negotiations tended to instigate a radicalization of demands made by the kidnappers in Lebanon, apparently due to fear that their share in a prospective deal might be neglected. Thus they threatened to kill hostages, and stressed that there could be no solution to the hostage issue unless Shi'ite detainees were released by Kuwait as well as by Israel. This stance was encouraged by the radical Iranian former interior minister, Ali Akbar Mohtashemi, who spoke publicly in Tehran as well as during a visit to Lebanon at the end of 1989, against any resolution of the hostage issue. The position enunciated by the semi-official *Tehran Times* on March 25, 1990, calling for the release by Israel of "thousands of Muslim prisoners," including Sheikh Obeid, may mirror the pressure exercised by extremist elements in Tehran and by the kidnappers in Lebanon.[25]

The circumstances which led, in April 1990, to the release of two American hostages were not at the time entirely clear. They appeared to have been linked primarily with alleged contacts between Washington and Tehran, as well as with Iranian and Syrian short-term interests. As in previous instances, Hizballah's interests and related stance appeared only secondary.

(For evidence of Iranian state-sponsorship--but non-Shi'ite perpetration--of the midair bombing of PanAm flight 103 over Scotland in late 1988, see Chapter 5, following.)

### Shi'ite Terrorism against Israeli and Jewish Targets

Shi'ite terrorism against Israeli and Jewish objectives has been concentrated primarily in Southern Lebanon and on Israel's northern border. Hizballah militiamen, organized in military formations and instructed by Iranian Revolutionary Guards stationed in Lebanon and by Syrian-backed Amal militia, have attacked IDF units in Lebanon since the aftermath of the 1982 war. The attacks have included suicide assaults, carbombs, and the planting of roadside explosive charges and mines, as well as frontal assaults on IDF targets and posts manned by the Israeli-sponsored Southern Lebanese Army. Hizballah has also initiated Katyusha attacks on Israel's northern border.

Since the IDF withdrawal from Lebanon in 1985, most of the attacks have been concentrated in or near the Israeli-declared Security Zone in Southern Lebanon. Israel holds pro-Iranian elements in Lebanon responsible for the detention of three Israeli soldiers captured by Amal and Hizballah on February 17 and October 16, 1986.

Members of the Jewish community in Lebanon have also been targeted by Shi'ite terrorism. Twelve Lebanese Jews have been kidnapped by Hizballah in Lebanon since 1984, most of them during March 1985. By May 1990 two or three Jews were still held hostage, while the remaining Jewish hostages had been executed, allegedly in retaliation for Israeli air raids on Shi'ite villages.

A principal core of Shi'ite antagonism toward Israel is the presence of IDF troops on Southern Lebanese soil and the backing provided by Israel to the primarily Christian-commanded Southern Lebanese Army. All told, however, Israeli and Jewish objectives have not been a frequent target of Shi'ite terrorism in the international arena. This low profile may be at least partially linked with Shi'ite interests in the Lebanese arena.

Moreover, in spite of the anti-Israel ideology advocated by Iran and Hizballah, lack of concrete Iranian interest in challenging Israel through the use of terrorism may have contributed to the relatively low volume of terrorist assaults perpetrated throughout the years against Israeli objectives abroad. Incidents that did involve Israeli and Jewish targets have usually been of the more general anti-western type--they were directed also at American and French targets. In any event, most of the schemes to attack Israeli targets were thwarted.

In 1985 the Islamic Jihad claimed credit for a bombing attack on an El-Al office in Istanbul, Turkey, and for several attacks against Jewish, Israeli and American targets in Scandinavia. However it later became known that most of the attacks in Scandinavia had been perpetrated by the Palestinian Popular Struggle Front (PPSF). The arrest in Italy in January 1987 of a Hizballah member carrying explosives thwarted plans to attack Jewish schools, a Jewish newspaper editor and a Jewish museum in that country.[26] A group of Hizballah members arrested in Turkey later that year had intended to attack American and Israeli diplomatic facilities.[27]

A terrorist apparently acting on behalf of Hizballah was killed in a London hotel on August 3, 1989 while handling an explosive charge. The Israeli consulate was mentioned by investigators as one of several possible targets of the planned attack, perhaps in retaliation for the capture by Israel of the Shi'ite Sheikh Abd al-Karim Obeid in Lebanon a few days earlier.[28] That event was also considered a probable motive for the assassination of Dr. Joseph Wybran, the leader of the Jewish community in Brussels, Belgium on October 3, 1989. It was alleged that the murder had been carried out by members of Abu Nidal's FRC at Iran's behest.[29]

## Conclusions

The involvement of Shi'ite militants in international terrorism since the Islamic Revolution in Iran is a complex phenomenon of many dimensions. Its association with state sponsorship of international terrorism has been the focus of this survey.

Iran and Libya have been actively supporting Middle Eastern terrorist groups operating in the international arena since the '80s; Libya and Syria were active already in the seventies. Since mid-1986 Syria and Libya have reduced the scope and volume of their direct involvement in international terrorism, primarily as the result of a firm response on the part of western states, as well as of developments related to domestic conditions and to the Israeli-Palestinian issue. Iran, on the other hand, has maintained an active involvement in international terrorism. Nevertheless, a relative decrease was evident in the volume of Shi'ite international terrorism during 1988 and 1989. This may be attributed to domestic developments in Iran, which in the summer of 1988 culminated in the conclusion of the Gulf War. The subsequent impression that Tehran was interested in rehabilitating its relations with the West was reinforced following the death of Khomeini in 1989, and the election to the presidency of Hashemi Rafsanjani. Yet it appears that the use of terrorism for extortionist or retaliatory purposes was still strongly advocated by dominant elements within the regime.

Several terrorism-related instances clearly attest to this inclination. In 1988 Iran was directly involved in the 16-day long hijacking of a Kuwaiti airliner, during which two of the passengers were murdered. In general, the operational acumen and sophisticated modus operandi displayed in hijacking incidents by Shi'ite terrorists attest to the special training and logistics provided by Iran.

Iran continued to be directly involved in the detention of at least 11 western hostages by Hizballah in Lebanon, with officials in Tehran publicly linking their fate to concrete aspects of Iran's relations with the West. The dramatic repercussions of the Rushdie affair clearly attested to the extensive influence of revolutionary Iran's message over militant elements all over the world.

Iran is suspected of directing the most lethal terrorist attacks carried out during 1988 and 1989: the midair bombings of a PanAm airliner over Scotland on December 21, 1988 and of a French UTA flight over the Sahara on September 19, 1989. Radical Palestinian elements were held responsible for the operational aspect of these incidents, against the backdrop of the intensification of their ties with the regime in Tehran. Operational cooperation between Hizballah and Palestinian groups was evident in the past mainly in the Lebanese arena, and as part of the struggle against the IDF in Lebanon. This new evidence of Palestinian-Iranian links was thus a source of concern to the West--the traditional victim of terrorist attacks orchestrated by both Palestinian and Shi'ite elements in the past. (The association between Iran and radical Palestinian elements is surveyed in detail in chapters five and six of this volume.) Finally, internal actors in Iran who advocated the use of terrorism remained influential, while even the so-called "moderate" camp identified with President Rafsanjani renounced terrorism neither in word nor in deed. More Shi'ite international terrorism sponsored by Iran could thus be anticipated.

The Shi'ite terrorist infrastructure deployed in the Middle East and elsewhere around the globe renders the translation of Iranian radical ideas into operational terms feasible. Hizballah cells apparently remained active in Western Europe, with Western Africa reportedly becoming a rear base for attacks against Western Europe. Another source of concern may be the relative independence occasionally displayed by Shi'ite terrorist cells, especially in Lebanon. Activity there, as well as in the Gulf states, is not always fully controlled by Tehran. This has been particularly salient in a few instances relating to the foreign hostages in Lebanon. In contrast, in Persian Gulf countries Shi'ite terrorist cells frequently appeared to lack the basic conditions crucial for the conduct of large scale terrorist campaigns.

For Iran, terrorism has proved to be a successful means of achieving specific national objectives on the international scene. Here a principal factor has been the reaction of the targeted states toward extortionist demands. They have made concessions despite their awareness of Iran's direct involvement in terrorism. When they have reacted, it has apparently not been firmly enough to deter Tehran from involvement in additional terrorism. Thus, despite the freezing of Iran's financial assets in American banks in 1979, the expulsion of Iranian diplomats from diverse capitals on charges of terrorism, and the termination of diplomatic relations with Tehran, Iran managed to pressure France into making significant concessions on the diplomatic, financial and political levels (yet was unable to prevent French weapons systems being delivered to Iraq); it gained US-made weapons as part of the arms-for-hostages deals; and it proved its capacity to detain foreign nationals in Lebanon for long periods of time, leaving almost no military rescue option. In some incidents Shi'ite terrorism has been successful in achieving the liberation of convicted terrorists from prison, although many Shi'ite terrorists were still detained in different countries by early 1990.

Measures taken directly against the Shi'ite terrorist infrastructure have included the crackdown on Hizballah cells in Europe in 1987 and the arrest of Amal member Fawaz Yunis by American FBI agents in September 1987. The latter instance involved implementation of the "long arm" provision (NSDD 138) of 1984, and was aimed against international terrorism involving Americans.[30] On several occasions, when the US administration perceived that lives of American hostages in Lebanon were in acute danger, it ordered the deployment of aircraft carriers, both opposite Lebanese shores and--in an attempt to deter Hizballah and Iran--in Persian Gulf waters. Yet when viewed in the context of American efforts to enhance the release of hostages, these measures never constituted more than a demonstrative show of force.

57

In May 1987 the US administration initiated a
"devaluation" policy vis-a-vis the hostage issue. This
attempt to relegate the kidnappings from the status of a
central political problem to a relatively marginal issue
was not always applied when international circumstances
appeared to mitigate a more traditional approach. Thus,
when Israel captured Sheikh Obeid, the administration
was led to upgrade the priority of the issue as a result
of a move initiated by another state.

By early 1990 American policy toward Iran, as defined by
the US State Department's Coordinator for Counter-
Terrorism, was based on diplomatic pressure directed at
isolation: "Iran continues to support terrorism from the
Middle East to Europe. And there is every indication
that this is state policy.... Until Iran acts to abandon
its policy...there will be no possibility of an
improvement in the US-Iranian relationship."[31]

Apart from this position, however (including American
refusal to expedite settlement of old financial debts to
Iran), the US did not evoke any concerted and
internationally-backed policy against Shi'ite
international terrorism sponsored by Iran. Under this
state of affairs Tehran appears to have assessed that
the political cost of reliance on terrorism by Iran and
its surrogates was tolerable. Yet one may speculate
that by 1990 key circles in Iran assessed that their
state support for terrorism was producing diminishing
returns.

# Notes

[1]M. Zonis and D. Brumberg, "Khomeini, the Islamic Republic of Iran and the Arab World," *Middle East Papers* no. 5, Harvard University, p. 75.

[2]A total of four hijacking incidents ended on Iran's territory.

[3]*Hadashot*, June 19, 1987; *Jerusalem Post* (*JP*), May 28, 1989 quoting *Observer*.

[4]*Nouveau Magasin*, June 4, 1988.

[5]*Maariv*, August 4, 1983; *US News & World Report*, November 10, 1986.

[6]*JP*, September 12, 1989 quoting *Reuter*.

[7]J. Kostiner, "The Rise and Fall of Militant Opposition Movements in the Arabian Peninsula," in A. Kurz (ed.) *Contemporary Trends in World Terrorism* (New York: Praeger, 1987), pp. 88-89.

[8]*Ibid*, p. 73; see also J. Goldberg, "The Shi'i Minority in Saudi Arabia," in J. Cole and N. Keddie (eds.), *Shi'ism and Social Protest* (New Haven and London: Yale University Press, 1986).

[9]International Herald Tribune (*IHT*), January 7, 1984.

[10]*IHT*, January 5, 1989 quoting *AFP*.

[11]*FBIS*, September 22, 1989 quoting *Riyadh TV*, September 21, 1989.

[12]*Washington Post*, April 15, 1985; *Counter-Terrorism*, February 9, 1987; *JP*, February 5, 1990 quoting *Sunday Telegraph*.

[13]This subject was the focus of M. Burgin, A. Kurz and A. Merari, *Foreign Hostages in Lebanon*, JCSS Memorandum no. 25, August 1988; as well as of M. Burgin, "Foreign Hostages in Lebanon--an Update," in *Inter: International Terrorism in 1988*.

[14]*Newsweek*, June 23, 1986 and May 16, 1988; *IHT*, December 26, 1986 quoting *Reuter*; *Le Monde*, May 6, 1988; *JP*, December 2, 1987 quoting *AFP*.

[15]*IHT*, January 31, 1990.

[16]*Ha'aretz*, February 24, 1987; *IHT*, January 19, 1987 quoting *New York Times* (*NYT*).

[17]*JP*, September 22, 1989 quoting *L'Express*.

[18]*IHT*, December 15, 1989 quoting *NYT*.

[19]*Ha'aretz*, October 30, 1983.

[20]*JP*, November 21, 1989 quoting *Paris Match*.

[21]*US News & World Report*, November 10, 1986.

[22]*NYT* December 25, 1986.

[23]*Al-Shiraa*, September 4, 1989; *Hadashot*, October 16, 1989 quoting *Al-Akhbar*, October 15, 1989; *Al-Ittihad*, October 24, 1989; *IHT*, March 5, 1990; *Independent*, March 11, 1990.

[24]*NYT*, October 24, 1989; *FBIS*, October 31, 1989 quoting *Tehran Times*, October 25, 1989.

[25]*Ha'aretz*, March 26, 1990 quoting *AFP*, *Reuter*.

[26]*Ha'aretz*, February 24, 1987.

[27]*Ma'ariv*, April 10, 1987.

[28]*JP*, August 6, 1989.

[29]*Ibid.*, December 11, 1989.

[30]D.C. Martin and J. Walcott, *Best Laid Plans: The Inside Story of America's War Against Terrorism* (New York: Harper and Row, 1988), pp. 156-157.

[31]Morris D. Busby, quoted in *Counter-Terrorism in the 1990's* (US State Department, January 1990).

# 5. The International Dimension of PFLP-GC Activity

The Popular Front for the Liberation of Palestine--General Command (PFLP-GC) is one of the Palestinian organizations known for their unequivocal rejection of any kind of political settlement with Israel, and their reliance on international terrorism to thwart any political process. The PFLP-GC's dependence on radical state sponsors increases the likelihood that it will react violently to any successful political process associated with the Israeli-Palestinian conflict.

Even beyond the confines of the Palestinian issue, the PFLP-GC retains both the motivation and the capacity to operate in the international arena. On December 21, 1988 PanAm flight 103 exploded in midair over Lockerbie, Scotland. While Iran was thought to have initiated that spectacular attack, the PFLP-GC was the major suspect in carrying out the operation.

In this chapter we shall attempt to illuminate the profile of the PFLP-GC, concentrating on its international dimension.

### Historical Background

The Syrian-sponsored PFLP-GC has been headed by Ahmed Jibril, a former officer in the Syrian Army, since its establishment in 1968. Jibril himself had been active in the Palestinian struggle against Israel since 1959, when he established his first group--the Palestine Liberation Front. Jibril has testified in several interviews that the PLF carried out its first assault against Israel in 1965. In 1967, the group merged with the Popular Front for the Liberation of Palestine (PFLP), headed by Dr. George Habash. But the alliance did not last long. The following year, the pro-Syrian Jibril split with the PFLP against the backdrop of mounting tensions between Habash and Damascus that led to Habash's arrest in Syria, and in view of policy differences: unlike Habbash, Jibril rejected any involvement in politics and advocated pure armed struggle.

Jibril now formed the PFLP-GC. Though a member of the PLO from the start, Jibril's organization consistently opposed the PLO's gradual shift toward a political orientation that was advocated mainly by Arafat's Fatah. The first sign of this shift was in June 1974, at the 12th meeting of the Palestinian National Council (PNC) in Rabat, when a decision was made to abandon international terrorism and to accept the establishment of a national authority in any liberated part of Palestine. Jibril signed the 10-point document summarizing the PNC decisions, but rejected the implication of the resolution--the readiness to make concessions in terms of territory and tactical preferences. The PFLP-GC did, however, comply with the decision to halt international terrorism, and from 1974 until the mid-'80s dramatically lowered its international profile. At the same time it joined the Palestinian rejectionist front, comprising the leftist Palestinian organizations that opposed the PLO's political shifts. Another move by the PFLP-GC was its withdrawal from the PLO Executive Committee and Central Council, although not from the PNC. In 1977, with the convening of the 13th PNC, the PFLP-GC reoccupied its seat on the PLO's Executive Committee. At that time, the stalemate in the Middle East political process and Arafat's advocacy of a more militant line in effect temporarily enabled Jibril to rejoin the PLO.

At about this time an internal conflict generated a schism within the ranks of the PFLP-GC. A group headed by Mahmud Zeidan (Abu al-Abbas) and sponsored by Iraq left the organization and established the Palestine Liberation Front (PLF). The direct cause for the split was Jibril's support for moves conducted by Syria in 1976 against the Palestinians in the civil war in Lebanon.

Jibril's close links with Syria led him in May 1983 to support a Syrian-backed mutiny that erupted within Fatah ranks in Lebanon. The mutiny reflected the opposition of radical factions within the PLO to another shift toward a political process led by Arafat. In December 1983 this struggle culminated in Arafat's flight from Tripoli, Lebanon, where he had sought to rebuild his military base following the expulsion of Fatah from Beirut in September 1982. At this time Syria established the Fatah Rebels, led by Muhammad Said Musa (Abu Musa), and Jibril broke with the PLO. In 1985, the Abu Musa group and the PFLP-GC joined the Palestine National Salvation Front (PNSF), created in reaction to the rapprochement between Fatah and King Hussein of Jordan. The accord signed between Arafat and Hussein that year was aimed at furthering a political process in the Middle East, and was categorically rejected by those Palestinian organizations that still advocated all-out war against Israel. Nor did the enmity between Jibril and Arafat end following the cancellation in 1986 of the accord and the subsequent stagnation in the regional political process.

From 1988, political moves made by Arafat against the backdrop of the Palestinian popular uprising in the Israeli-administered Territories again emphasized the discrepancies between the positions of Jibril and the PLO. Jibril totally rejected the recognition by Arafat of UN resolutions 242 and 338 and his renunciation of terrorism. He accused Arafat of abandoning the PLO credo, and in 1989 participated in Iranian-sponsored efforts to create a new organization that would replace the PLO.

By 1990 the PFLP-GC remained outside the PLO. But Jibril's tightening links with Iran generated internal opposition within his organization. Led by the PFLP-GC's former representative in the PLO Executive Committee, Talal Naji, this faction advocated rejoining the PLO and lobbying from within against Arafat's line, and opposed the shift toward Iran. The political bureau of the Front reached a compromise resolution, according to which collaboration with Tehran would continue, yet Naji could veto political decisions that contradicted his views. This agreement appeared to have temporarily prevented a split within the PFLP-GC.

The organization, which in 1990 had about 800 members, was based in Syria. It maintained bases near Damascus, in the Syrian-controlled Biq'a and in the coastal region of Lebanon, near Damur. Until late 1989 it had bases and personnel in Libya as well, but at that time Qadhafi ordered the expulsion of the organization from the country.

## Ideology and Strategy

The fundamental themes guiding the activity and intra-Palestinian political path of the PFLP-GC are pan-Arabism, a total rejection of Israel's right to exist, and advocation of armed struggle as the only way to advance the Palestinian cause. Hence it has devoted its activity solely to armed struggle, while dissociating itself from any political course.

Jibril is aware of the Palestinians' limited military capabilities. He regards Palestinian armed activity against Israel as a mere catalyst or vanguard force in the fight for the liberation of Palestine, to be followed by a war led by Arab states. He also claims that the unity of the Arab world will be achieved through the struggle for Palestine. The process will be fulfilled in the elimination of Israel and the establishment of a Palestinian state from the Jordan River to the Mediterranean Sea.

Jibril attributes a major role to the Palestinian armed struggle in disrupting any chance for a negotiated settlement to the Israeli-Palestinian conflict. An important role attributed to terrorism according to this perception is that of turning both Israeli and Palestinian moderate forces into extremists. Therefore he adheres to the ideas articulated in the PLO charter regarding the strategic role of the armed struggle, and totally rejects the acceptance by the PNC of the possibility of territorial concessions, even within the framework of the strategy of stages. Jibril vehemently denounced the declaration by Arafat at the 19th PNC in November 1988 of a Palestinian state in the Territories alongside Israel.

The PFLP-GC is stereotypically termed a Marxist-Leninist organization. Jibril defines his struggle as a war against "imperialism" and "colonialism" as embodied in Israel. In his speeches, he advocates a popular struggle aimed at destroying the "roots of reaction." The United States is considered an enemy of the Palestinian people due to its support for Israel and the role it plays in mediating between Israel and the Arab world. Official contacts between the US administration and the PLO after late 1988 naturally increased the Front's antagonism toward the US.

An interesting shift in the PFLP-GC mindset took place in 1988, when this secular Arab organization entered into collaboration with Iran. Although the turn to Iran was primarily motivated by pragmatic considerations, it also reflected Jibril's perception of the changing political balance of power in the region. Realizing that Syria and Libya had succumbed to western pressures to cease their support for terrorist groups, Jibril saw in the new Islamic force a more powerful backer for the organization's struggle against the West, and particularly the US. As Arabism had proved to be too weak a driving force in the struggle for the liberation of Palestine, Jibril hoped that "victorious Islam" would achieve more. Accordingly, Jibril's ideological messages were now enriched with Islamic phrases. On March 5, 1989 he pledged to carry out "the Islamic verdict, to protect Islam and its prophet," against Salman Rushdie, author of *The Satanic Verses*.

Jibril's new-found tendency toward Islam is particularly interesting in that, unlike other Palestinian organizations, including those on the Left, Jibril has no specific vision of the future nature of the Palestinian state. Nor is the PFLP-GC's struggle against Israel restricted to any specific front, whether cross-border, inside Israel or abroad. However, while action against Israel on Israeli soil is motivated purely by the goal of armed struggle, activity abroad is also directed toward serving the interests of a supportive state.

65

Because Jibril has rarely publicized his concept of the operational course of the PFLP-GC, the few declarations he did make may be of some significance. In September 1982 he announced that the PFLP-GC would escalate the struggle against Israel, and threatened that this would not be restricted to the "occupied territories but rather [will be carried out] in all international arenas where the enemy and its allies' institutions and interests can be found." This declaration, which followed the withdrawal of the Palestinian organizations, including the PFLP-GC, from Beirut, expressed the Front's vision of the ceaseless struggle against Israel, and its readiness to shift bases and operational arenas. A more explicit warning was issued in February 1986, when Jibril threatened "any passenger thinking of using Israeli or American airliners." This declaration was made in response to Israel's interception of a Syrian airliner flying from Libya. It was reportedly Ahmed Jibril whom Israel had hoped to capture in that airliner.

### Links with States

A principal strategic policy of the PLO has been its rejection of any attempt by a foreign country to influence the Palestinian decisionmaking process ("freedom of decision"). The PFLP-GC, while vowing adherence to these guidelines, was never reluctant to form close relationships of dependency with a foreign state. A major reason for this approach has been the organization's opposition to any political settlement to the Israeli-Palestinian conflict. This in effect has released the PFLP-GC from preoccupation with a variety of political considerations beyond those involving intra-Palestinian matters.

Throughout the years, the PFLP-GC has maintained links of varying degrees of intensity with three Middle-Eastern countries--Syria, Libya and Iran--that share its adherence to the rejectionist line. As a result, the Front engaged in terrorist activity, mainly in the international arena, as a proxy, serving the national interests of the sponsored state rather than necessarily those of the Palestinian national cause.

**Syria** has provided the organization with arms, finances, and bases since its formation. The organization's two major camps are located in the vicinity of Damascus, while activists are also stationed in the Syrian-controlled Biq'a in Lebanon, from where cross-border attacks against Israel have been initiated.

Beginning in 1985 Syria directed a world-wide terrorist campaign aimed at sabotaging the agreement reached that year between Jordan's King Hussein and Yasir Arafat. Elements that participated in that campaign were Syrian-state agents, as well as extremist Palestinian organizations, the most active of which was Abu Nidal's Fatah Revolutionary Council (FRC). Operatives of the PFLP-GC were also allegedly involved in a related series of attacks, presumably in association with, or by activating members of, the Palestinian Popular Struggle Front (PPSF). Assaults carried out during 1985 that were attributed to PPSF members took place in Scandinavia and the Netherlands, and targeted Jewish, Israeli and American objectives. The head of Syrian military intelligence, Ali Duba, was said to have activated the cells involved in the attacks. Ali Duba was reportedly also involved in the establishment in early 1987 of the PFLP-GC infrastructure in West Germany and Sweden. Cells of the organization operating in those countries were uncovered in October 1988.

During 1987 Syria significantly reduced its financial support to the PFLP-GC. This move was taken on the grounds of economic difficulties, but may have also been the result of pressure applied to Syria during 1986-1987 by the West. In response, Jibril turned to Libya and Iran seeking financial support and logistical backing.

Still, the association between Syria and the PFLP-GC appears to remain a fundamental one that is not influenced by ephemeral issues. Even when the organization has operated at the behest of Libya or Iran, it sought Syrian approval for its associations and activities. Ali Duba himself was reported to have been involved in contacts between the PFLP-GC and Libya, when the latter was searching for a proxy to carry out retaliatory attacks against the US following the April 1986 American air raid against military and terrorist targets in Tripoli and Benghazi. Syria also apparently approved of the active PFLP-GC role in the December 1988 bombing attack against the PanAm airliner, which was directed by Iran.

Cumulative evidence linking the PFLP-GC to the PanAm explosion brought about appeals by the US to Assad to expel the organization from Syria. Syria has been under pressure to dissociate itself from international terrorism since late 1986, when the US and other western states applied diplomatic and economic sanctions following the disclosure in a London court of its direct involvement in a plot to bomb an El Al airliner. Nevertheless, beyond a few symbolic measures, Syria did not sever its ties with the groups it sponsored. This, for example, was the case when Abu Nidal was ordered to remove the headquarters of his organization from Damascus as a result of American pressure applied to Syria: in 1987 the FRC merely moved to a Syrian-controlled area of Lebanon.

Relations between the PFLP-GC and **Libya** have intensified as Syria has bowed, however symbolically, to sanctions imposed by western states. The links had in fact been established earlier--in 1983 Qadhafi arranged to train members of the PFLP-GC and other terrorist organizations in Bulgaria. Since 1986, Libya has provided the PFLP-GC with funds and logistical bases.

An important factor in the relationship between the Front and Libya was the organization's participation in the war in Chad. Libyan Air Force officers trained PFLP-GC pilots for combat aircraft, and the latter took an active part in the war in Chad. According to reports from September 1987, one of them was downed over Ndjamena, capital of Chad, while flying a Libyan Tupolev-22 bomber. Jibril claimed that in 1987 the relationship between his organization and Libya became unilateral: his men were fighting for Libya in Chad, but Qadhafi ceased supplying the Front with money or logistical support. However Libya was reported to have paid the organization for carrying out the December 1988 bombing assault against the PanAm airliner at the behest of Iran. Moreover, in 1987 Libyan government-owned companies reportedly bought hang gliders for the PFLP-GC in France.

In 1989 Qadhafi publicly renounced international terrorist activity, declaring these attacks to be counterproductive to the Arab cause. Libya's relations with Arafat's PLO mainstream have since improved, while his ties with extremist Palestinian elements have deteriorated. Thus Jibril was ordered in September 1989 to close his offices in Tripoli, and Front members were reported to have moved to Damascus.

Links between the PFLP-GC and **Iran** became closer in December 1987, when Ahmed Jibril met with Iranian Foreign Minister Ali Akbar Velayati in Tripoli, Libya, and conveyed his support "for the Islamic Revolution." The relationship that has developed since then has apparently produced political as well as operational manifestations.

Thus Jibril took part in an Iranian attempt to create "an Islamic organization for the liberation of Palestine," aimed at replacing the PLO. First steps in this direction were made in April 1988, when representatives of the PFLP-GC, the FRC and the Palestinian Islamic Jihad discussed the subject in Libya. In September 1989 a major conference was held in Tehran to discuss plans for escalating the struggle against Israel. The meeting was chaired by Velayati; participants included Ahmed Jibril, leaders of the Iranian-sponsored Hizballah, a leader of the Lebanese Sunni militia Tawhid, and Abu Musa. A call for the establishment of a "formal Palestinian-Iranian alliance" was issued by Jibril in December that year.

An alliance of this sort was in fact formed in late 1988 between the PFLP-GC, the FRC, and Hizballah. It was reported that high ranking Hizballah activists had discussed with the PFLP-GC plans to bomb American and French targets. Yet by April 1990 this coalition--which

69

presumably was directed by Iran--had still not found operational expression in the international terrorist arena. We have noted that the developing links between Iran and the PFLP-GC aroused internal opposition against Jibril. This may have affected the scope of collaborative activities.

The role of the PFLP-GC as a proxy for Iran was apparently manifested in the most demonstrative way in the bombing of PanAm flight 103. It is generally believed that the bombing attack was carried out in retaliation for the accidental downing by an American naval cruiser of an Iranian airliner over the Persian Gulf on July 3, 1988, and that it was but one in a series of attacks planned by the organization at the behest of Iran. The PFLP-GC reportedly received a large sum of money from Iran and Libya in payment for perpetrating the operation, in addition to a monthly financial stipend. Throughout 1989 and early 1990 western security agencies made intensive efforts to unequivocally uncover the identity of the sponsors and perpetrators. Meanwhile, cumulative evidence linked the PFLP-GC to the attack. One of the most substantive indications was the discovery, on October 26, 1988 and in March 1989, of three explosive devices similar to the one presumably used in the PanAm incident, in the possession of a PFLP-GC cell captured in West Germany.

The PFLP-GC was also suspected of perpetrating the midair bombing of the French UTA airliner on September 19, 1989 over Niger. That incident, too, was presumed to have been carried out on behalf of Iran. According to French sources, the explosion involved the same kind of device as those found with the PFLP-GC members arrested in West Germany. French officials also claimed that shortly before the attack, PFLP-GC operatives held talks with pro-Iranian elements in Beirut and discussed schemes to deter France from activating its naval force deployed off the Lebanese shore, against the backdrop of the confrontation between Syria and General Aoun's forces. Another probable cause for Iranian revenge against France was the latter's alleged failure to fulfill its part of a deal concluded with Tehran in

1987, whereby it was to pay Iran in return for the release of French hostages held by Hizballah.

The links between the PFLP-GC and Iran bear a dangerous potential. This is an association between a well-organized group dedicated to armed struggle, and a state that is relatively insensitive to world criticism and sanctions. However, because they are based upon pragmatic considerations, the relations are vulnerable to two potential sources of change: internal opposition within the organization to its links with Iran, and/or Syrian pressure upon Jibril to halt his involvement in international terrorism and to cut his links with Iran. This could happen, for example, in the event of a shift in the relationship between Iran and Syria.

### Coordination with Additional Terrorist Organizations

There are few indications as to operational links between the PFLP-GC and other terrorist groups. This is most probably due to the organization's preference through the years for close relationships with sovereign states that provided it with logistical assistance. States were also involved in some of the alliances formed between the PFLP-GC and other organizations, such as Hizballah and the FRC.

In June 1986 Jibril indicated that his organization maintained links with the Japanese Red Army (JRA). The JRA has also been associated with the PFLP, and has been supported by Libya. For three successive years after 1986 it carried out attacks against American and other western state targets that coincided with the anniversary of the American air raid against Libya. A Japanese newspaper reported in November 1989 that a JRA operative, known as a personal acquaintance of Qadhafi, delivered explosives to a "senior member" of the PFLP-GC in Budapest, Hungary.

On September 20, 1988 the Red Army Faction (RAF) attempted to assassinate Hans Titmeyer, the West German finance minister. It claimed responsibility for the attack under the name "Khaled Aker Unit." Aker, a member of the PFLP-GC, was killed on November 25, 1987 during an attack on an IDF base in the north of Israel. There was no further evidence linking the PFLP-GC to the RAF in general or to this incident in particular. At the time of the attack, however, a PFLP-GC operational infrastructure already existed in West Germany. Thus it is a matter of conjecture whether the solidarity between the two organizations expressed in the claim of responsibility by the RAF reflects a certain level of cooperation.

In late 1989 it was reported that the PFLP-GC had established a network of dormant operatives and arms caches in cooperation with the Provisional Irish Republican Army (PIRA) in West Germany, the Netherlands and Sweden. A British journalist reported that as part of the logistical collaboration between the organizations, a PFLP-GC cell in Germany supplied PIRA with the Kalashnikov assault rifle used in an attack on a British soldier's wife in September 7, 1989 in Dortmund, West Germany.

Links with foreign terrorist organizations are not a crucial element in PFLP-GC operational capacity, as it is apparently able to function with the assistance provided by supportive states. Its essentially military orientation also renders it indifferent to ideological solidarity as a basis for links with foreign organizations.

### International Infrastructure and Activity

The PFLP-GC has operated in the international arena since the early 1970s. All told, the volume of its activity in this sphere has been low: by April 1990 the list of international incidents attributed to the organization comprised some 26 actual and attempted attacks. Yet most of these were highly sophisticated operations. They reflected considerable technical expertise, as well as an inclination toward dramatic and lethal attacks. The first international terrorist incident carried out by the organization was the midair bombing on February 21, 1970 of a Swissair airliner destined for Israel, killing all 47 passengers and crew. From then until August 1980, the organization was involved in nine international terrorist attacks, most of which were foiled. Two explosive charges planted aboard airliners did go off, and three additional attempts were thwarted. Also intercepted were attempted bombings, parcel-explosives, a scheme to attack an Israeli target in Denmark, and a plane hijacking.

During the early '80s, no activity by the PFLP-GC in the international arena was recorded. When it resumed international operations in the mid-'80s, this was not motivated solely by a drive to escalate the Palestinian struggle against Israel, as was the case in the 1970s. This time, the PFLP-GC served interests alien to the Palestinian cause.

Clearly, the heyday of PFLP-GC international activity was in the early 1970s. We have noted that the 12th PNC's decision in June 1974 to cease international terrorism was accepted by Jibril, although it did not completely end Front activity abroad. However, after 1974 the Front shifted the focus of its operations to attacking Israel directly across its borders, including occasional barricade-hostage and mass-killing attacks.

During these years, as well as in the 1980s, the Front did not operate squads within Israel. Its presence inside the Territories has also always been relatively insignificant; since 1974, less than a dozen incidents inside Israel have been recorded.

Similarly, activity in the international arena has remained limited quantitatively. We have noted that during 1985-1986 persons linked with the PFLP-GC-- albeit not members of the organization--were involved in terrorist activity perpetrated in Denmark, Sweden and the Netherlands. During the years 1987-1989, Front operatives were directly involved in four international attacks.

PFLP-GC activity abroad is facilitated by an infrastructure in Western-Europe. It was not dismantled as the Front reduced its involvement in international terrorism in the 1970s, and dormant cells were maintained in several countries. Locations for European bases were selected on the basis of the relative freedom of movement provided by the authorities for Palestinian operatives in certain states. Another important factor was the presence of a Palestinian community.

Thus, members of the organization were active in Greece and in Malta, though only as logistical and exit bases for operatives, based on the authorities' laxity toward the presence of Palestinian operatives there. The geographical proximity of Malta to Libya made it even more attractive, and PFLP-GC members who lived there frequently traveled to and from Libya. The bomb used in the PanAm explosion was apparently concealed in a suitcase and sent on its fatal journey from a base in Malta.

An operational base was also established in Yugoslavia. In an apartment in Krusevac, near the Italian border, police found an arms cache consisting of Semtex explosives, Soviet-made TNT, hundreds of detonators, and lengths of fuse wire. Police investigators in Yugoslavia believe that bombs found in possession of the PFLP-GC cell in West Germany were constructed with materiel supplied from the Yugoslav arms cache.

The PFLP-GC also established bases in Sweden and West Germany. In both countries there are large communities of Palestinians seeking work or political asylum that constitute a potential reservoir for recruitment of operatives and a base for assistance and refuge.

In 1987 a 34-member cell of the PFLP-GC was established in West Germany by Hafez Dalkamoni, the organization's head of operations in Western Europe. He entered West Germany early that year on a Syrian passport, and based himself in Dusseldorf. The local authorities became aware of the existence of the cell in September 1988, and put the suspected terrorists under telephone surveillance. During the period until their arrest, contacts were made between members of the cell and members of the PPSF living in Sweden, some of whom had been involved in terrorist attacks in Scandinavian states during 1985-1986. Muhammad Abu Taleb, leader of the Swedish cell, and Marten Imandi, a member of it, were apparently linked to the Dalkamoni cell.

On October 26, 1988, when evidence gathered by the West Germany security authorities indicated that the West German cell was about to act, a major sweep of the hideouts of the cell's members was carried out. Fourteen activists were detained, 12 of whom were released shortly thereafter. Hafez Dalkamoni and another Palestinian remained in custody. The arrests provided information on previously unsolved attacks perpetrated in Germany. According to Dalkamoni's confession, he had already carried out two bomb attacks on US military trains: on August 31, 1987 a bomb just missed a military train near Hedemunden; and on April 26, 1988 a US military train traveling from Kessel to Goettingen was hit.

In the apartments of the detainees, including Dalkamoni's, police seized arms, explosives and barometric fuses. The most interesting find was a radio-cassette player loaded with explosives, and activated by a barometric fuse. In March 1989 the German police found two similar devices in the apartment of Dalkamoni's brother-in-law, a Palestinian who had acquired German citizenship and lived in Neuss. The arrest of the cell, however, did not prevent the disaster of the PanAm incident scarcely two months later, though it undoubtedly foiled additional planned attacks.

The disclosure of links between Palestinians from Sweden and Dalkamoni's cell led to the detention of six Palestinians in October 1988 in Uppsala. However, they were released shortly thereafter. In May 1989 the Swedish police swept several apartments in three cities and detained suspects, of whom four were charged and sentenced for a series of bomb attacks carried out in Copenhagen on July 22, 1985 and in Stockholm on April 6, 1986 against Jewish, Israeli and American targets. The four, members of the PPSF, included Muhammad Abu-Taleb and Marten Imandi. As we have seen, these two had tangible links with the Dalkamoni team in West Germany.

It now emerged that Abu-Taleb had traveled in October 1988 to Malta to organize the PanAm bombing together with Dalkamoni, who was also in Malta at the time.

As noted earlier, too, the October 1989 attack against the UTA airliner allegedly involved a charge that consisted of a Semtex explosive concealed ' in a radio-tape player, similar to those found in West Germany.

The Front acquired important reinforcements when members of the May-15 organization joined its ranks. May-15 was established by Muhammad Al-Amri, alias Abu Ibrahim, who was notorious for his expertise in bombmaking. May-15 was dissolved in 1985 and its members joined Fatah and the PFLP-GC. Although the PFLP-GC already possessed basic know-how in the construction of sophisticated bombs, it may be presumed that the former May-15 members contributed their experience in preparing the sophisticated charges found in possession of the West European network a few years later.

## Conclusions

PFLP-GC involvement in terrorism has two major foci. The organization has been active in Southern Lebanon and has occasionally staged cross-border infiltration attempts into Israel. At the same time it maintains an infrastructure abroad. While activity along Israel's borders falls within the framework of the Palestinian armed struggle, activity in the international sphere involves interests and implications that go beyond the Israeli-Palestinian conflict.

Activities at the behest of a foreign power have been a principal characteristic of the PFLP-GC since it resumed operations on the international scene in the second half of the '80s. Yet intra-Palestinian frictions and the Israeli-Palestinian conflict remain a driving force behind the organization. Thus, its present low volume of activity in the international arena is linked with developments associated with both background factors.

The political process generated by the *intifada* has evoked sharp condemnation by Palestinian leaders opposing Arafat and the PLO. Jibril has openly attacked all parties concerned: Israel, the US and the PLO. He is thought to have a prime interest in halting the political process. Yet by mid-1990 the organization had not resorted to a concerted terrorist campaign aimed at demonstrating its rejection of the political moves advocated by the PLO mainstream. This was probably linked with the rather unique origins of the current process.

Traditionally, the PFLP-GC and other groups and states that oppose the very notion of a negotiated solution in the Middle East have focused their criticism and activity on the PLO, and particularly on Arafat. The situation generated by the *intifada* was different. The Declaration of Independence by the 19th PNC was to a large extent a response by the PLO to the wishes of the Palestinian populace in the Territories as expressed by the Unified National Leadership of the Uprising. Opposing it meant confronting not only Arafat and the PLO, but also the very essence of the Palestinian uprising.

Another reason for the low profile of international activity by the PFLP-GC in 1989-90 derived from the organization's association with Syria. Since late 1986 Damascus has been under international pressure to refrain from direct involvement in blatant acts of international terrorism. This placed an additional constraint on Jibril's inclination to operate in the international arena.

All told, the probability that the PFLP-GC would resume large-scale international terrorist activity seemed to depend upon two interrelated factors: the extent of militancy of Iranian foreign policy, and Syria's readiness to tolerate its client's potential for getting it into embarrassing situations. By mid-1990, the shadow of the PanAm affair appeared to be restraining both Iran and the PFLP-GC. The results of the official investigation of the case could bear significant ramifications for the future activity of the Front.

# 6. Palestinian International Terrorism in 1989

A relatively small number of international terrorist assaults were attributed to Palestinian elements in 1989.

- On January 16 a letter bomb was defused at the Israel Embassy in London. Responsibility for the attempted bombing was claimed by the previously unknown "January 15" group, believed to be associated with the Islamic Jihad.

- The same group claimed responsibility for the planting of explosive charges that were discovered and defused on June 3, at the American and British cultural centers in Cairo.

- The PFLP-GC was allegedly involved in the September 19 explosion over the Sahara in Niger of a UTA airliner en route from Congo to Paris, in which 171 people were killed. While Shi'ite elements were also suspected of carrying out the bombing, this did not rule out a possible PFLP-GC role.

- On October 3 Dr. Joseph Wybran, a prominent leader of the Jewish community in Belgium, was shot to death by a lone gunman in Brussels. The assassination was attributed to Abu Nidal's FRC.

- The FRC also carried out the October 6 abduction of two Swiss Red Cross employees in Ein al-Hilwe, Lebanon. The kidnappers demanded the release from Swiss jail of a Shi'ite who had hijacked an Air Afrique airliner to Geneva in 1987. It was alleged that the abduction had been perpetrated on behalf of Hizballah. By June 1990 the two were still held captive.

- In December four Palestinians suspected of plotting terrorist attacks were arrested in Cyprus.

This list of incidents illustrates the two main features that characterized Palestinian international terrorism during 1989. For one, the volume of activity was marked by a dramatic decline. Further, actual assaults and additional developments related to the international infrastructure of Palestinian terrorism were accompanied by a considerable measure of ambiguity as to the concrete backdrop of incidents and the organizational affiliation of those involved in attacks. These features form a striking contrast with previous years' Palestinian terrorist activity in the international sphere--when spectacular incidents associated with the Palestinians preoccupied the agendas of world leaders and public figures, and Palestinian organizations vied to claim responsibility for attacks.

***Factors that Affected Palestinian International Terrorism***

A decrease in international incidents perpetrated by Palestinians was already evident in 1987. It was mainly attributed to policy changes by the radical organizations' sponsoring states, following punitive and deterrent measures conducted by the affected countries. Another factor that produced this lower profile was the freeze in the Middle East political situation that prevailed prior to the outbreak of the *intifada*.

Among the groups most influenced by their sponsoring states' political considerations and readiness to risk association with international terrorism, was Abu Nidal's FRC--one of the most active agents of international terrorism during the year preceding this shift of trend.

Alternations in FRC operational tactics, and a corresponding reduction in the organization's international activity, were already evident in late 1986. These were mainly the result of external constraints, particularly a reduction in Libyan leader Qadhafi's declared support for insurgent organizations that followed the mid-1986 American air raid on Libya,

79

and the lowering of Syria's profile of direct involvement in international terrorism since late 1986.

Additional factors that presumably produced a reduction in FRC international activity were intra-organizational. In 1987 Abu Nidal promised to halt terrorist activity in the international arena for a period of ten months, as part of a new strategy aimed at positioning himself closer to the mainstream of the Palestinian national movement and leadership. When this period ended in mid-'88, elements of the organization made a spectacular comeback to the international arena (for details, see *InTer 1988*.) By then, the entire framework of the Palestinian struggle had changed due to the outbreak of the uprising in the Territories, and the assaults were perpetrated to manifest dedication to the armed struggle. But the campaign generated friction within the group's ranks, focusing on the issue of the future course of the fight; this culminated by late 1989 in a series of intra-organizational assassinations in Lebanon and Libya, causing several prominent members to leave the FRC. All this took place against a backdrop of rumors concerning Abu Nidal's terminal illness, his worsening relationship with Qadhafi, and his house arrest by the Libyan ruler.

Additional developments during 1989 that formed at least a partial explanation for the low volume of Palestinian terrorism in the international sphere, were linked with the counterterrorism drive conducted by western states, including a series of interceptions of terrorists. Some of these were linked with the intensive efforts to clear up the mystery surrounding the explosion in December 1988 of PanAm flight 103 over Scotland. The resultant disclosures did not provide conclusive evidence concerning the actual initiators and perpetrators of the incident. But they did lead to revelations concerning the Palestinian terrorist infrastructure in Western Europe.

Several of those arrested were linked with Palestinian terrorist activity in Scandinavia. Of five Palestinians captured in May in Sweden, some allegedly were associated with the PanAm attack: they were linked with members of Jibril's PFLP-GC detained in West Germany on grounds of involvement in that incident. Four of the persons arrested in Sweden were sentenced in December 1989 for participation in attacks against Jewish and American targets that had been carried out in the mid-'80s in Sweden, Denmark and the Netherlands. One of those convicted still faced charges linking him to the PanAm incident. The incidents perpetrated in the mid-'80s were attributed to the PPSF; therefore the organizational affiliation of the convicted terrorists as well as the nature of operational links between the two radical groups remained unclear. Two previous discoveries in Sweden were the October 1988 arrest in Upsala of five PFLP-GC members, and the capture that summer of an arms cache allegedly belonging to the FRC, near the Stockholm airport.

A Danish group of 11 persons, allegedly involved since the early 1980s in carrying out robberies for the PFLP, was uncovered in April 1989. Also captured were an arms cache and a 'hit list' comprising 500 potential targets, including Jewish figures and Danish institutions and persons. Eight people were charged in Denmark in October 1989 for gathering this information. Yet actual plans for attacks, if there were any, were not specified.

This series of arrests in Scandinavian countries was marked by considerable ambiguity regarding the links among groups and the organizational affiliation of the detained persons. Conceivably, some of these associations were established on the grounds of personal acquaintanceship, and did not necessarily follow directives issued at higher echelons of the groups. The existence of a large Palestinian community in Scandinavia presumably facilitated the establishment of a terrorist infrastructure there. Years before actually being activated, Palestinians affiliated with radical groups may have lived there and prepared the groundwork for attacks.

Additional terrorism-related arrests took place in Italy. A network of the PPSF was uncovered in September in southern Italy and its members accused of association with the Mafia. It was alleged that the Palestinians supplied the Mafia with arms in return for safehouses and arm caches. An Abu Nidal operative, who was also associated with the Red Brigades, was arrested in early September, but released several weeks later.


## Potential Threats

These interceptions of terrorist cells and related revelations reflected the existence of a Palestinian international infrastructure. This, coupled with indications of the nature of the associations linking the radical groups and the major sponsors of Middle Eastern international terrorism--Syria, Libya and Iran-- appears to corroborate the assessment that future activity in this arena by Palestinian elements is both feasible and probable.

Turning to a specific look at state sponsors of Palestinian terrorism, **Syria** undertook a significant reduction in the volume of its operative involvement in international terrorism. Yet its ties with radical organizations operating in the scene were not cut, and active connections with the international infrastructure of groups were maintained.

The same can be said for **Libya**. Reacting to pressures imposed on him during 1989 by the PLO and Egypt, Libyan leader Qadhafi apparently revised his policy of sponsoring revolutionary organizations. He publicly announced a halt to support for groups perceived as harming the Arab cause. In an interview given in late October to an Egyptian paper, Qadhafi declared that skyjackings and attacks against non-combatants were murderous acts that ill suited the goals of the struggle; therefore he had cut Libyan assistance to the groups involved. Earlier, in September, he noted that radical Palestinian groups would in future receive Libyan assistance only through official Palestinian channels such as the Red Crescent. By early 1990 it was reported that Qadhafi had ordered the removal of PFLP-GC bases from Libya.

Declarations aside, however, the picture of Libyan attitudes remained ambiguous. Meetings among radical Palestinian groups--including the PFLP-GC, Abu Musa's faction of the Fatah and the PPSF--were held in 1989 in Libya, and the establishment of an alternative organization to the PLO was discussed. In April the Libyan media expressed support for unspecified terrorist intentions to attack American targets on the occasion of the third anniversary of the American air raid against Libya.

**Iran** has been cautious regarding direct association with international terrorist incidents and their perpetrators. But its links with Shi'ite and Palestinian organizations have not been kept secret. As Syria's and Libya's self-imposed restrictions on direct involvement in international terrorism have increased during 1988-89, Palestinian ties with Iran have tightened.

According to reports from late 1989, the PFLP-GC was receiving a monthly payment from Iran. A widely accepted allegation also linked that organization to the execution, on behalf of Iran, of the attack against PanAm flight 103. The operation was said to have been initiated by Iranian former interior minister Mohtashemi, and was meant to avenge the downing of the Iranian airbus in July 1988 by the US. Additional allegations held that Qadhafi had taken part in planning the attack, and delivered to the PFLP-GC part of the money paid for the operation. In any event the PFLP-GC established logistical bases in Iran. The organization also established links of a possibly operational nature with the Iranian Revolutionary Guards. On March 7, 1989 Ahmed Jibril pledged to "work to execute Islamic law against Salman Rushdie," and British security services were put on alert for a terrorist squad made up of revolutionary guards and members of the PFLP-GC that reportedly was set up to carry out Khomeini's verdict against the writer.

Reports from 1989 also indicated closer links between Iran and the FRC. That organization maintained operational links with Hizballah in Lebanon, and in late

1988 both organizations, together with the PFLP-GC, reportedly formed a common rejectionist front. A joint operations apparatus, "Soldiers of Truth," was said to have been established by the FRC and Hizballah. Although collaboration between the two organizations was probably intended to serve the interests of both in the Lebanese arena, it nevertheless implied that a closer relationship had been established between Iran and the Palestinian radical group--one that could be manifested outside Lebanese territory as well. It was in fact speculated that the October 1989 assassination of a prominent Jewish leader in Belgium was carried out by the FRC in retaliation for the abduction by Israel of a prominent Shi'ite leader, Sheikh Obeid, from Southern Lebanon. By late 1989 it was reported that FRC terrorist teams had left their bases in the Lebanese Biq'a and moved to Europe to carry out attacks against Saudi objectives there.

## Future Prospects

Any attempt to assess the likelihood of terrorism in the future is difficult, because of the multiplicity of factors presumably involved. These may range from intra-organizational developments, through changes in the nature of links between groups and sponsoring states and the effects of countermeasures conducted by the affected countries, to political processes at regional and global levels. Yet an assessment is possible of situational causes that may stimulate the activation of existing logistical infrastructures and networks of associations among radical elements.

Whenever a political process was underway in the past, diverse Palestinian factions and their sponsoring states have had to address both the possibility of their own participation--and the converse issue of the form of their opposition. In this sense, it may be argued that renewal or stagnation of the Middle East political process might alter considerations of radical Arab states regarding the potential harm that involvement in terrorism could cause to their international prestige. Alternatively, these developments could produce pressures from within the organizations to launch fresh terrorist attacks.

Two major developments during the past two years could delay the renewal of an all-out terrorist campaign directed by radical Arab states. One is the popular uprising or *intifada* in the Israeli-administered Territories; the other is the changing reality in Eastern European states.

The eruption of the *intifada* reinforced the political path advocated by the mainstream of the Palestinian nation and leadership. In so doing it changed the political backdrop for terrorism by radical Palestinian factions. It triggered a major regional political process, and this in turn raised speculation concerning the possibility of renewed terrorist campaigns to be carried out with the aim of frustrating progress toward a negotiated settlement.

Yet this sort of resort to blatant terrorist acts in reaction to political developments that terrorism is unlikely to halt, may be perceived by radical Arab states as too costly. They might also be influenced by the new political disposition of the Eastern Bloc countries, and the USSR in particular, as these countries have backed Arafat's political initiatives. Indeed these Eastern Bloc political positions are being translated into practical constraints on the perpetration of international terrorism. In 1989 the rapprochement between the US and the USSR led to discussions and an official agreement on cooperation in combatting terrorism. At a minimum, reversal of the Eastern Bloc's longtime policy of active assistance to revolutionary elements will probably result in mounting logistical limitations on the activities of local and foreign extremists in Western Europe and beyond.

Still, in anticipation of future political moves, further attacks could be expected to be carried out against Israel, additional states involved in the process, and pragmatic Palestinians. Assaults by rejectionist elements could also be aimed at fostering doubts, if not concerning the PLO's genuine intention to reach a peaceful solution, then at least regarding its ability to control extremists and thereby guarantee the implementation of a future negotiated agreement.

In the face of restrictions on the scope and volume of terrorist activity imposed by Arab states, and the effect of changing policies of Eastern European countries, radical elements might seek logistical aid elsewhere. Two possibilities in Western Europe are criminal elements and local terrorist organizations. This apparently explains the motivation for the reported creation, in 1989, of a joint "sleeper" network of activists and arms dumps in Western Europe by the PFLP-GC and the Provisional Irish Republican Army. An Iranian role in facilitating activity perpetrated by Palestinian elements in the international arena also remained viable. Yet at least some of the attacks conducted by Iranian-sponsored groups would appear to be detached from the Palestinian cause and concurrent developments in the Middle East political process.

Finally, a word about the likelihood of a concerted comeback by the PLO mainstream to the arena of international terrorism. By early 1990 prospects for such a development seemed remote. The organization's leadership obviously recognized that acts of international terrorism could jeopardize efforts to benefit politically from the uprising in the Territories and hamper its drive to acquire an active role in the regional political process. The renunciation of terrorism not only had its diplomatic benefits; it also, according to PLO spokesmen, involved actual attempts to foil other Palestinian groups' activities in the international arena. In order to curb activities considered harmful to Palestinian interests, Fatah has in effect cooperated with western states' security agencies and offered assistance in uncovering the perpetrators of spectacular attacks. Yet the PLO's reluctance to condemn the deadly attack perpetrated in February 1990 against Israeli tourists on Egyptian soil, as well as the PLF attack on Israeli beaches in June 1990, proved again that PLO diplomacy cannot be detached from its internal political considerations.

# 7. CHRONOLOGY OF MAIN TERRORIST INCIDENTS IN 1989

## January 4 - Bangkok, Thailand

Salah al-Maliki, a third secretary in the Saudi Embassy, was shot to death by a lone gunman. The Soldiers of Justice, believed to be a joint apparatus of Abu Nidal's Fatah Revolutionary Council (FRC) and Hizballah, claimed responsibility in Beirut. A pro-Iranian Hizballah branch in Saudi Arabia, using the name Islamic Jihad Hejaz, also claimed responsibility for the incident.

Radical Shi'ite elements were held responsible for an intensive terrorist campaign carried out throughout 1988-1989 around the globe against Saudi diplomats. The attacks were presumably linked with the death of Iranian pilgrims to Mecca during clashes with the Saudi security services on July 31, 1987. Another allegation suggested that the anti-Saudi incidents were perpetrated in retaliation for the September 31, 1988 execution by Saudi authorities of pro-Iranian Shi'ites convicted of terrorist activity. It was also alleged that the attacks were in fact designed to jeopardize a rapprochement between Iran and Saudi Arabia, and reflected a power struggle in Iran between moderates and hardliners. These attacks are included below chronologically.

## January 16 - London, England

A letter bomb sent to the Israeli ambassador in London was safely defused. Responsibility for the attempted bombing was claimed by the January 15 organization, believed to be affiliated with the Palestinian Islamic Jihad (JI).

*January 27 - Ankara and Istanbul, Turkey*

Extensive damage was caused in three coordinated bomb attacks against US business concerns: the Turkish-American Businessmen's Association and the Economic Development Foundation--both in Istanbul, and the Metal Employees' Union in Ankara. The targeted buildings were sprayed with Leftist slogans before explosive charges were detonated. The Dev Sol (Revolutionary Left) was held responsible for the attacks.

*January-November - Pakistan*

A series of bombing attacks against the Pakistani public-at-large that began in 1987, continued throughout 1988 and 1989. It was attributed to Afghani agents. Following are key incidents perpetrated during the year under review:

*January 11 - Peshawar, Pakistan*

Four persons were killed and 13 wounded when a bomb exploded at a bus stop.

*February 2 - Quetta, Pakistan*

Three people were killed and five wounded when a bomb exploded at a bus stop.

*April 19 - Karachi, Pakistan*

At least 16 people were injured when a bomb exploded aboard a bus.

*July 4 - Peshawar, Pakistan*

Ten people were killed and 29 injured in a bomb attack on a bus passing through a crowded market.

*July 17 - Mardan, Pakistan*

A device planted under the fuel tank of a bus destroyed eight other buses and part of the station but caused no casualties.

*July 17 - Punjab, Pakistan*

Six people were injured in a powerful blast at a railroad workers' housing area.

*August 6 - Peshawar, Pakistan*

Five people were killed and another 31 injured in a bomb explosion at a vegetable market.

*August 8 - Peshawar, Pakistan*

Two persons were killed in a bomb explosion at a hotel.

*September 13 - Peshawar, Pakistan*

A bomb blast ripped through a hotel restaurant, killing five and injuring 22.

*September 18 - Peshawar, Pakistan*

A bomb exploded aboard a minibus, killing three people and injuring two.

*October 18 - between Wazirabad and Gujarat, Pakistan*

A bomb exploded aboard a bus, killing eight people and injuring 30.

*November 13 - Peshawar, Pakistan*

A bomb exploded in a hotel room, causing damage but no casualties.

*November 24 - Peshawar, Pakistan*

A bomb exploded under a car, killing two passersby.

### *January-October - Spain*

The Basque Euskadi Ta Askatasuna (ETA) repeatedly attacked French targets in protest against the expulsion from France of ETA members since June 1986. The incidents also came in retaliation for a series of arrests of ETA members in France. The incidents usually targeted French automobile showrooms, but other objectives were targeted as well. Following are key incidents perpetrated during 1989:

*January 8-9 - Logorno, Spain*

Two French car showrooms were attacked with bombs.

*April 27 - Lasarte, Spain*

Minor damage was caused when a bomb exploded at a Michelin tire factory.

*May 9 - Bilbao and Zarauz, Spain*

A Renault car showroom was attacked with two bombs.

*May 24 - Bilbao, Spain*

A car dealership was bombed.

*May 25 - Bilbao, Spain*

A bomb went off at a Renault car dealership.

*August 15 - near Bilbao, Spain*

A car dealership was attacked with a bomb.

*September 18 - Bilbao, Spain*

A Renault car dealership was bombed.

*September 27 - Bilbao, Spain*

Peugeot and Citroen car dealerships were bombed.

*September 27 - Bilbao, Spain*

A bomb was defused at a Renault car dealership.

*October 1 - near Bilbao, France*

Two car dealerships were bombed.

*October 14 - Biarritz, Cibourne and Saint Jean de Luz, France*

Significant damage was caused when bombs exploded in a dry cleaning business, on a French police boat and at a Socialist Party office.

## January-December - Colombia

The 500 mile Cano-Limon oil pipeline, jointly operated by Colombia's National Oil Firm together with Ecopetrol, Occidental and Shell oil companies, was the target of a bombing campaign that accounted for several dozen incidents during the year. The series of attacks, perpetrated by the Ejercito de Liberacion Nacional (ELN), caused damage estimated at $15 million dollars to the pipeline that moves crude oil from Crauo Notre oil field near the Venezuelan border to the Caribbean coast. The ELN has repeatedly called for the nationalization of Colombia's oil industry and the expulsion of foreign oil companies. During 1989 the ELN called a halt to attacks against the pipeline, and therefore the volume of the campaign was low compared with previous years' rates.

## *February 11 - Cologne, Federal Republic of Germany*

Two people, apparently members of the Iranian opposition, were injured when a bomb went off outside a university building. The blast appeared to have been carried out by pro-Iranian terrorists, who targeted a meeting of an Iranian opposition group.

## *February 14 - Tehran, Iran*

Ayatollah Ruhollah Khomeini issued a death sentence against the writer Salman Rushdie for allegedly blaspheming Islam in his book, *The Satanic Verses*, published in Britain. The call to execute the novelist created an international furor and temporarily halted the process of rehabilitating Iranian links with the West. It was also followed by a series of threats and bombing attacks. The incidents, however, were minor and non-lethal (with one exception--see event of March 29, below). They were primarily intended to cause property damage and intimidate owners of bookshops and publishing houses involved with distributing the novel. Related attacks were carried out in Pakistan, the US and Western Europe--mostly in Italy, France and the UK. It is believed that the spate of bombings was perpetrated by local Muslims.

### February 18 - near Comayagua, Honduras

Three US soldiers and two Honduran bystanders were injured when an explosion ripped through a bus carrying the troops to their base. The incident was attributed to Fuerzas Popular Revolucionario Lorenzo Zalaya (FPRLZ).

### February 27 - Bogota, Colombia

A bomb exploded at the entrance of the Summer Institute of Linguistics, injuring three American citizens. Responsibility was claimed by the Ejercito Popular de Liberacion (EPL).

### March 10 - San Diego, USA

A vehicle belonging to the US Navy captain who commanded the American cruiser *Vincennes*, which downed the Iran Air jetliner on July 3, 1988 over the Gulf, was destroyed in a bomb explosion. The captain's wife, who was driving the vehicle, escaped unharmed. Responsibility for the attack was claimed by the Guardians of the Islamic Revolution, believed to be a cover name for pro-Iranian or Iranian agents.

### March 10 - Athens, Greece

Extensive damage was caused when an explosive charge went off in a French bank. Responsibility for the attack was claimed by Revolutionary Solidarity (SR), which is believed to be associated with the Epanastatikos Laikos Agonas (ELA). The statement issued by the organization expressed solidarity with members of Action Directe (AD) imprisoned in France.

## March 29 - Brussels, Belgium

The Saudi Imam of a Brussels mosque, Abdallah Ahdal, and his Tunisian deputy, Salim Bahri, were shot to death. Responsibility for the incident was claimed by the Soldiers of Justice, believed to be a joint apparatus of Abu Nidal's FRC and Hizballah. The assassination was apparently carried out in retaliation for the Imam's moderate stand regarding the novel *The Satanic Verses*.

## April 9 - Manila, Philippines

An American communications relay facility was damaged in a bombing attack. This was the first time in recent years that terrorists have actually penetrated a US military installation. In another, foiled attempt, landmines were laid in a road frequently used by Clark Air Base personnel. Both attacks were considered part of New People's Army (NPA) efforts to disrupt negotiations between the US and the Aquino government concerning the extension of American rights to use military installations in the Philippines, set to expire in 1991.

## April 9 - Ramal de Aspusana, Peru

Two *Newsweek* reporters were abducted and interrogated by the Sendero Luminoso (SL). They were released after three days in captivity.

## April 21 - Manila, Philippines

A US Army colonel was shot and killed on his way to work. The NPA, which claimed responsibility for the assassination, threatened to carry out further attacks against Americans involved in Aquino's counterinsurgency effort, if her government did not close American military bases in the Philippines.

94

*April 26 - near Medellin, Colombia*

One Spanish and two Italian engineers, working at the Rio Grande Hydroelectric Dam, were abducted. The EPL was held responsible for the kidnappings. By early 1990, the fate of the victims remained unclear.


*May 8 - Luanda, Angola*

Extensive damage was caused and two persons were injured when a bomb went off at the offices of several foreign oil companies. The National Union for the Total Independence of Angola (UNITA) claimed responsibility for the attack, and detailed the targets: Texaco, USA; Petromar, France; and Sumitomacorp of Japan.


*May 24 - La Paz, Bolivia*

The Left-wing Zarate Willca Armed Forces of Liberation (ZWFAL) claimed responsibility for the killing of two Mormon missionaries in protest against foreign interference in Bolivia. The incident was part of an anti-Mormon campaign conducted throughout Latin America. Most of the attacks were minor and resulted in no casualties.


*May 28-29 - Larnaca, Cyprus*

Six men bearing Lebanese passports were arrested in Cyprus on suspicion of plotting to assassinate the Lebanese Christian leader General Michel Aoun. The Syrian Social Nationalist Party (SSNP) claimed responsibility for the attempt.

## June 3 - Cairo, Egypt

Two explosive devices were safely removed from the grounds of the American and British cultural centers. The January 15 organization, which was also held responsible for the letter bomb sent to the Israeli ambassador to London in January, was considered the main suspect. Other suspects were the Egypt Revolution organization, which was involved in carrying out attacks against US and Israeli targets throughout 1984-1986, and the Nasserite Organization, which was responsible for attacks perpetrated against British and American objectives in 1988.


## June 18 - Hungary

Soviet Army headquarters was set on fire and an unknown number of soldiers were injured.


## June 19 - Osnabruck, Federal Republic of Germany

A bomb explosion at a British Army barracks caused extensive damage but no injuries. Five additional explosive devices planted at the site were found and defused. The Provisional Irish Republican Army (PIRA) claimed responsibility for the incident, which occurred five days after the indictment of two of the organization's members jailed in Osnabruck.


## June 20 - Brussels, Belgium

Samir Jah al-Rasul, a Saudi Embassy employee, was shot to death. Pro-Iranian elements, using the name The Free People of Arabian Peninsula, claimed responsibility for the assassination in a statement released in Beirut.

*July 2 - Hannover, Federal Republic of Germany*

PIRA claimed responsibility for a carbomb attack in which a British serviceman was killed and members of his family injured. A second explosive device left in a nearby car was safely defused.


*July 10 - Mecca, Saudi Arabia*

A Pakistani national was killed and 16 people were wounded in two blasts near the Grand Mosque in Mecca during the annual pilgrimage. Pro-Iranian elements, using the name Generation of Arab Rage, claimed responsibility for the attack and stated that the blasts constituted a warning to the Saudi royal family. Sixteen Kuwaitis, allegedly members of the Followers of the Line of the Imam (i.e., Imam Khomeini in Iran), were executed in September for carrying out the attacks. Threats to retaliate for the execution were issued by several pro-Iranian elements.


*July 13 - La Ceiba, Honduras*

Seven US soldiers were wounded by a grenade outside a discotheque. The Morazanist Patriotic Front (FPM) claimed responsibility for the incident.


*July 14 - Saint Avold, France*

Two Irishmen and an Irish woman, in possession of marked maps and explosives, were arrested on suspicion of plotting attacks to be carried out in the Federal Republic of Germany, to coincide with the August 20th anniversary of the British military presence in Northern Ireland.

## August 3 - London, England

A terrorist was killed at a hotel while preparing a bomb. Pro-Iranian elements, using the name Mojahiddin of Islam, claimed responsibility in Beirut, saying that the man had been planning an attack against the British author Salman Rushdie. It was also suggested that the mission was directed by Hizballah, in protest against the capture of the prominent Shi'ite leader Sheikh Abd al-Karim Obeid in July in Southern Lebanon by Israel.

## August 23 - Istanbul, Turkey

An explosive device exploded near the Israeli Consulate, causing no damage or injuries. The Armed People's Units, believed to be associated with the Marxist Kurdish Workers Party (PKK) claimed responsibility for the attack. There may have been a link between the incident and anonymous calls received at the Israeli consulate, promising to avenge the abduction of Sheikh Obeid.

## August 28 - Hannover, Federal Republic of Germany

An attempt by PIRA to blow up the car of a British military officer was foiled.

## September 1 - Munster, Federal Republic of Germany

Two British soldiers in a military housing complex were shot. PIRA claimed responsibility in Dublin, threatening further assaults against British government and military targets worldwide.

## September 7 - Dortmund, Federal Republic of Germany

The West German wife of a British soldier was shot to death while sitting in a parked car. PIRA claimed responsibility for the incident, which marked the first time a non-British citizen was killed by the organization in West Germany.

## September 19 - over Sahara, Niger

A French UTA airliner, en route from Brazzaville, Congo to France, crashed less than an hour after it took off from a stopover in Chad. All 171 passengers and crewmen aboard were killed. By early 1990, the identity of the perpetrators remained unknown. The principal suspects, however, were Shi'ite and Palestinian elements.

Responsibility for the attack was claimed by the Islamic Jihad, which linked it with an exchange of information between France and Israel concerning the detention by the latter of the Shi'ite leader Sheikh Obeid. It has been suggested that France's reluctance to fulfil obligations allegedly made in 1989 in return for the release of French hostages held by Hizballah in Lebanon may have formed the motive for the attack. A related assumption linked the explosion with efforts directed by radical Iranian factions to disrupt alleged negotiations concerning the fate of western hostages still held by Hizballah.

Allegations also focused on Palestinians as the perpetrators, in cooperation with or on behalf of Iran. The explosive device used in the bombing was similar to the one used in the December 21, 1988 bombing attack against PanAm flight 103 over Lockerbie, Scotland, for which the PFLP-GC has been held responsible. In view of the PFLP-GC's close links with Tehran, the possibility that the incident was a joint operation of Hizballah and Palestinians cannot be ruled out.

## September 20 - Baghdad, Iraq

Three hand grenades were hurled at a club serving as a meeting place for expatriates of many nationalities, injuring 25 persons. A claim of responsibility on behalf of the United Organization of the Halabjah Martyrs, possibly affiliated with Kurdish elements, was issued in Sidon, Lebanon. However, resemblance between tactical features of the incident and past attacks perpetrated by Abu Nidal's FRC, as well as the nature of the target, led observers to presume a possible involvement of Palestinian elements.

## September 26 - near Manila, Philippines

Two American Ford corporation employees were shot to death in an ambush. The NPA, which opposes the US military presence in the country, was held responsible for the attack.

## September 28 - Federal Republic of Germany

An attempt to blow up a British soldier's car was intercepted. PIRA was held responsible for the foiled attack.

## October 3 - Brussels, Belgium

Joseph Wybran, leader of the Jewish community in Belgium, was shot and killed. Responsibility for the murder was claimed in Tel Aviv on behalf of the previously unknown Direct Revenge. The Soldiers of Justice, believed to be a joint apparatus of Hizballah and Abu Nidal's FRC, claimed responsibility in Beirut, saying the victim was assassinated in retaliation for the assassination of an FRC member. The possibility that the attack was carried out by FRC at Iran's behest cannot be ruled out, against the backdrop of relations between the organization and Tehran.

## October 6 - Sidon, Lebanon

Two Red Cross technicians were kidnapped. Responsibility for the abduction was claimed by the Islamic Jihad. It has been alleged, however, that the kidnapping was carried out by FRC on behalf of Hizballah, in an attempt to force the release from Swiss jail of a Shi'ite who had hijacked an Air Afrique airliner to Geneva in 1987. By June 1990 the two were still held in captivity.

## October 13 - Seoul, South Korea

Six members of the Leftist Sochongyon, a radical student movement, hurled bombs at the US ambassador's residence, causing damage but no injuries.

## October 14 - Lahore, Pakistan

Damage was caused and several persons were injured in a bombing attack that targeted the offices of the Saudi airline.

## October 16 - Ankara, Turkey

A Saudi military attache, Abdel Rahman Shrewi, was seriously wounded when a bomb exploded in his car. A passerby was killed in the incident, and another injured. Hizballah, using the name Islamic Jihad, claimed responsibility for the attack and warned Saudi Arabia to expect revenge for the execution of 16 Kuwaitis found guilty of involvement in two bombings that took place in August 1989 in Mecca. The organization also demanded the release from Swiss jail of a Shi'ite terrorist accused of the 1987 hijacking to Geneva of an Air Afrique airliner. A Turkish terrorist group named Turkish Jundallah, considered responsible for the October 1988 murder of a Saudi diplomat in Turkey, was also suspected of carrying out the attack.

## October 22 - Cape Town, South Africa

An explosive device went off outside the headquarters of British Petroleum's South African subsidiary and caused damage. That same day another bomb exploded outside a BP gas station. The attacks were probably carried out by militant elements of the African National Congress (ANC) or the Pan African Congress of Azania (PAC), in protest against Britain's opposition to the implementation of economic sanctions on South Africa, advocated in a meeting of Commonwealth nations.

## October 24 - The Hague, Netherlands

An explosion near the house of a Spanish diplomat caused property damage but no casualties. The Basque ETA was held responsible for the attack, which was exceptional in terms of its geographical venue, since the organization usually confines its activities to Spain and southern France.

## October 25 - near Tripoli, Libya

An Italian national, a resident of Libya, was shot to death. The circumstances of the killing remained unclear, yet the backdrop was thought to be mounting tension between Italy and Libya following the blocking that day, in Naples port, of a Libyan cruise ship. The cruise passengers intended to observe a day of mourning declared by Qadhafi for Libyans deported during Italian colonial rule. Another possibility was that Muslim fundamentalists were behind the assassination: that month, a wave of attacks in protest against Libyan efforts to rehabilitate relations with the outside world was recorded in the country.

*October 26 - Munchen-Gladbach, Federal Republic of Germany*

A British soldier was shot to death.  Also killed in the attack was the soldier's child.  Responsibility for the attack was claimed by PIRA.

*October 27 - The Hague, Netherlands*

The offices of the commercial and labor attaches at the Spanish Embassy were targeted in bombing attacks. Responsibility for the incidents was claimed by the Basque ETA.

*October 30 - Manila, Philippines*

A US military intelligence agent was shot to death.  The NPA was held responsible for the assassination.

*November 1 - West Beirut, Lebanon*

A Saudi diplomat, Ali al-Marzuki, was shot to death and his driver wounded by gunmen firing from a passing car. Hizballah, using the name Islamic Jihad, claimed responsibility for the attack, declaring it was carried out in retaliation for the execution in September in Saudi Arabia of 16 Kuwaiti Shi'ites charged with planting bombs in Mecca during the July pilgrimage. Another alleged reason for the assassination was Hizballah's opposition to efforts made by Saudi Arabia and other Arab states to achieve a national conciliation in Lebanon.  On the same day the Saudi Embassy in the city was targeted in a bombing attack, for which Hizballah was also held responsible.

*November 4 - Copenhagen, Denmark*

The office of the US computer company Unisys was vandalized. No group claimed responsibility, but an anarchist Danish group, known as BZ, was held responsible by authorities for the attack.

*November 8 - Mindanao, Philippines*

Two Austrian engineers were killed and three wounded in an ambush by armed assailants. The Moro National Liberation Front (MNLF) was suspected of carrying out the attack.

*November 10 - Izmir, Turkey*

An explosive charge went off outside a US military PX. Dev Sol was held responsible for the attack.

*November 23 - over the Arabian Sea, Middle East*

A bomb was found aboard a Saudi airliner flying between Islamabad, Pakistan and Riyadh, Saudi Arabia and safely defused. Iranian-inspired or directed elements were suspected.

*November 24 - Huallaga, Peru*

An American reporter was kidnapped and turned over to drug traffickers, presumably in exchange for money. His body was found with a note indicating that the SL was responsible.

*November 27 - Bogota, Colombia*

A Colombian Avianca Airlines aircraft en route from Bogota to Cali exploded in midair. All 107 crewmen and passengers, including two US citizens, were killed. The Extraditables, a drug trafficking group, claimed responsibility for the explosion.

*December 6 - Bosphorus Straits, Turkey*

A bomb exploded aboard an unoccupied launch used by the US consular staff, causing extensive damage but no casualties. The attack was claimed by the previously unknown Warriors of the 16th June movement.

## December 6 - The Hague, Netherlands

Two grenades were launched at the residence of the Spanish ambassador, causing minor damage and no casualties. The attack was attributed to the Basque ETA.

## December 8 - Athens, Greece

An explosive device went off at an EEC office, causing damage but no casualties. An ELA communique sent to a local newspaper before the incident warned of the coming attack. The communique also praised the assassination by the Red Army Faction (RAF) of the German financier Alfred Herrhausen.

## December 9 - Antwerp, Belgium

A Belgian policeman, conducting a routine check at the port, was shot and wounded. The incident was believed to have been carried out by PIRA, although the Irish People's Liberation Organization (IPLO), a leftist Catholic group, was also considered to be possibly responsible.

## December 14 - Manila, Philippines

An explosion slightly damaged the house of the US Embassy's agricultural attache, injuring a Filipino workman. Earlier, two grenades were fired into the US Embassy residential compound, causing minor damage but no injuries. While no group claimed responsibility for the attack, allegations centered on rebel soldiers. Later on, two grenades were hurled at a building complex housing US Embassy workers, causing moderate damage.

## December 16 - Brussels, Belgium

Two hand grenades were found underneath the car of a Syrian diplomat and safely defused. Responsibility was claimed by the Syrian fundamentalist organization People's Mojahiddin, thought to be associated with the Muslim Brotherhood. This organization also claimed responsibility for the shooting of a Syrian diplomat on October 7, 1987 in Brussels.

# Organizations Responsible for International Terrorist Incidents in 1989

------------------------------------------------------------

Listed according to popular designation or acronym, full name or translation, and national affiliation of members. Some designation details are incomplete.

| | |
|---|---|
| Al-Amal | Shi'ite militia, Lebanon. |
| ANC | African National Congress, South Africa. |
| APU | Armed Peoples Units, Turkey. |
| AWB | Afrikaanese Weerstandsbeweging (The Afrikaner Resistance Movement), South Africa. |
| BR | Brigate Rosse (Red Brigades), Italy. |
| BZ | Full name unknown, Denmark. |
| CONTRAS | Anti-Sandinists, Nicaragua. |
| Dev Sol | Devmirci Sol (Revolutionary Left), Turkey. |
| ELA | Epanastatikos Laikos Agonas (People's Revolutionary Struggle), Greece. |

| | |
|---|---|
| ELN | Ejercito de Liberacion Nacional (National Liberation Army), Colombia. |
| EPL | Ejercito Popular de Liberacion (Popular Liberation Army), Colombia. |
| ETA | Euskadi Ta Askatasuna (Basque Fatherland and Liberty Movement), Spain. |
| Extraditables | A Narco-terrorist group, Colombia. |
| FMLN | Frente Farabundo Marti Para la Liberacion Nacional (Farabundo Marti Front for National Liberation), El Salvador. |
| FPM | Frente Patriotico Morazanista (Morazanist Patriotic Front), Honduras. |
| FPMR | Frente Patriotico Manuel Rodriguez (Manuel Rodriguez Patriotic Front), Chile. |
| FPRLZ | Fuerzas Popular Revolucionario Lorenzo Zalaya (Lorenzo Zalaya Popular Revolutionary Force), Honduras. |
| FRC | Fatah Revolutionary Council, Palestinian. |
| Hizballah | Shi'ite, Lebanon frequently used cover names during 1989: Free People of the Arab Peninsula, Generation of the Arab Rage, Guardians of the Islamic Revolution, Islamic Jihad, Islamic |

|  | Jihad Hijaz, Mojahiddin of Islam, Soldiers of Justice (believed to be a joint apparatus with Abu Nidal's FRC). |
|---|---|
| IPLO | Irish People's Liberation Organization, Northern Ireland, United Kingdom. |
| Iraultza | Revolution, Basque Armed Revolutionary Workers Organization, Spain. |
| JI (Palestinian) | Islamic Jihad, responsibility claimed under the name January-15. |
| JRA | Japanese Red Army, Japan. |
| Jundallah | (God's Warriors), Shi'ite, Turkey. |
| JVP | Janatha Vimukthi Peramuna (People's Liberation Front), Sri Lanka. |
| MB | Muslim Brotherhood, Syria. |
| MIR | Movimiento de la Izquierda Revolucionaria (Movement of the Revolutionary Left), Chile. |
| MJL | Movimiento Juvenil Lautaro, Chile. |
| MKO | Mojahiddin Khalk Organization, Iran. |
| MNLF | Moro National Liberation Front, Philippines. |
| MNR | Mozambique National Resistance Movement (Renamo), Mozambique. |

| | |
|---|---|
| MRTA | Movimiento Revolucionario Tupac Amaru (Tupac Amaru Revolutionary Movement), Peru. |
| Nasserite Organization | Egypt. |
| NLU | National Liberation Union, Surinam. |
| NPA | New People's Army, Philippines. |
| PAC | Pan African Congress of Azania, Lesotho/Swaziland. |
| PFLP | Popular Front for the Liberation of Palestine, Palestinian. |
| PFLP-GC | Popular Front for the Liberation of Palestine-General Command, Palestinian. |
| PIRA | Provisional Irish Revolutionary Army, Northern Ireland, United Kingdom. |
| PKK | Partiya Karkeren, Kurdistan (Kurdish Workers Party), Turkey. |
| POLISARIO | People's Front for the Liberation of Saguiat al-Hamra and Rio de Oro, Western Sahara, Morocco. |
| PSP | Progressive Socialist Party, Lebanon. |
| RARA | (Revolutionary Anti-Facist Action), Netherlands. |
| SL | Sendero Luminoso (Shining Path), Peru. |

| | |
|---|---|
| SNM | Somali National Movement, Somalia. |
| SPLA | Sudanese People's Liberation Army, Sudan. |
| SR | Social Resistance, Greece. |
| SSNP | Syrian Social Nationalist Party, Lebanon. |
| SWAPO | South West African People's Organization, Namibia. |
| TL | Terra Lliura (Free Land), Spain. |
| UNITA | Uniao Nacional para a Independencia Total de Angola (National Union for the Total Independence of Angola), Angola. |
| URNG | (Guatemalan National Revolutionary Unity), Guatemala. |
| Warriors of 16th June | Turkey. |
| ZWFAL | Zarate Willca Fuerzas Armadas de Liberacion (Zarate Willca Armed Forces of Liberation), Bolivia. |